W9-BVM-788

A POCKET MIRROR FOR HEROES

for

BALTASAR GRACIÁN

EDITED AND TRANSLATED BY

CHRISTOPHER MAURER

CURRENCY DOUBLEDAY

NEW YORK • LONDON • TORONTO • SYDNEY • AUCKLAND

A Currency Book

PUBLISHED BY DOUBLEDAY

a division of Bantam Doubleday Dell Publishing Group, Inc.

1540 Broadway, New York, New York 10036

Currency and Doubleday are trademarks of Doubleday,

a division of Bantam Doubleday Dell Publishing Group, Inc.

Book design by Julie Duquet

Library of Congress Cataloging-in-Publication Data

Gracián y Morales, Baltasar, 1601–1658.

[Selections. English. 1995]

A pocket mirror for heroes / Baltasar Gracián ;

edited and translated by Christopher Maurer.

p.   cm.

Contents: The hero—The beveled edge—The better part of discretion.

I. Maurer, Christopher.   II. Gracián y Morales, Baltasar, 1601–1658.

Héroe.   English.   III. Title.

PQ6398.G3A6   1995

868'.309—dc20   95-32754

CIP

ISBN 0-385-48021-0
Printed in the United States of America

January 1996

First Edition

1   3   5   7   9   10   8   6   4   2

CONTENTS

INTRODUCTION

A Pocket Mirror for Heroes is a book of stratagems for reaching excellence in a competitive world ruled by appearances and, often, deceit.

It is a *mirror* because it reflects "the person you are or the one you ought to be." A *pocket* mirror because its author took the time to be brief. A mirror for *heroes* because it provides a vivid image of ethical and moral perfection. For the author, a hero is "the consummate person, ripe and perfect: accurate in judgment, mature in taste, attentive in listening, wise in sayings, shrewd in deeds, the center of all perfection."

The author is Baltasar Gracián, a discerning, witty Spanish Jesuit best known for *The Art of Worldly Wisdom*, a collection of three hundred piquant aphorisms on prudent behavior, published in 1641 and received with much success in our own day.

Both books are briefs for wise living. But in *Worldly Wisdom* Gracián pushes brevity to extremes. Even his syntax is pared to the bone: "The good, if brief, twice good; the bad, if little, less bad!" It is rewarding, but not always easy, to decipher those three hundred points of prudence: the reader must match wits with the author to fathom his meaning and unravel his paradoxes. And many will be grateful for the more discursive style of *A Pocket Mirror*. Drawing on a greater variety of literary forms—not only the aphorism but also dialogue, essay, letter, fable, and allegory—Gracián conjures up extremes of stupidity and wisdom, generosity and envy. With equal intensity he ponders life's pitfalls and possibilities. Convinced that he is living "at the tail end of the centuries," and that it is harder than ever to reach greatness, he offers "a compass for sailing toward excellence," "an art for reaching distinction."

Drawing on four of his works, *A Pocket Mirror* gives us a more "unbuttoned" Gracián: just as brilliant, just as avid for perfection, but funnier, more playful, less guarded. These pages prove him a companion for "all seasons, all hours": welcome company for anyone who recognizes, but also relishes, the challenges of daily life.

For Gracián, those challenges are considerable: the world can be a deceitful, dirty, and dangerous place. Life itself begins as a dupe: who, he asks, would have knowingly inherited a treasure entailing so much misery? Since we have, we must proceed with caution, adapt to circumstance, take nothing for granted. Acknowledging the difficulties of life, Gracián imagines us "stuck in the mud from which we were formed," but reminds us, with a sigh, that, despite everything, "there is nothing to do but go

To reach that acuity, Gracián draws on an unshakable belief—uncommon in our own time—in the power of art and artifice. Life with others may indeed be "warfare," a *"milicia contra la malicia"* (militia against malice); but art rescues us with stratagems, tested by generations of the wise and available to anyone willing to interrogate the right authors, converse with the right people, and turn the pages of human experience. Art, too, is an enchantress, Gracián writes. But whereas Circe turned men into pigs, art turns us fully into people. Only art and artifice and the spark of wit allow the "discreet," the "prudent," the "well-advised," to succeed at any of life's daily challenges: choosing friends and finding the time to learn from them; identifying the job best suited to one's character; conquering one's moods; knowing what to conceal and what to reveal to others; and "sweetening" the truth so that we can teach and not offend.

In Gracián's world, no "rules," no "instructions," no set of "habits," lead directly to success. Rules are inflexible; no book of instructions will ever compete with the randomness of human activity; and any "habit" or pattern of behavior makes us predictable and therefore vulnerable to others: it is "easy to shoot the bird that flies in a straight line," or defeat the person who always plays his cards in the same manner. What Gracián scrutinizes in *A Pocket Mirror* are the ethical and moral *qualities* that have led to success. Those qualities are constants in wise behavior, but they are anything but absolute values; like the maxims in *The Art of Worldly Wisdom*, each is "a point of departure for individual reflection."[3] The qualities must be carefully appraised, adapted to one's surroundings, combined to their best advantage, displayed in the right manner, and sometimes "counterfeited." Timidity can pass for caution; rashness for courage; self-doubt for humility; inconsistency for verve and spontaneity. And when nature has begrudged us good qualities, artifice can produce synthetic ones; most people do not care whether courtesy is "natural" or "artificial": they simply enjoy it. Even a fool can hide under a cloak of silence. Only the wise are able to distinguish a quality from its shadow, decipher the text of life, "balance the accounts of truth."

Gracián's belief in the importance of appearances is one of the most strikingly modern aspects of his writing. For him it is a melancholy fact of life that fools outnumber the intelligent. They are noisily "infinite," and a large part of their foolishness lies in an inability to move beyond appearances to what lies within. The importance of appearances is, for Gracián, crucial; they are not merely the "rind" that one peels away and disposes of in order to get to the essence of things. The rind is as essential as the fruit; *both* must be dealt with. Whether or not they should, people do judge a book by its cover and a monk by his cowl, and both the cover and cowl must be made as attractive as possible and displayed in the right light: perhaps in *half*-light, so as to awaken mystery or at least curiosity. We depend upon appearances for knowledge and, like it or not, can know things and people only "from the outside in." Best, then, to dress for success, and to study the entire wardrobe of virtue and vice.

In his fable about the Peacock (pages 145–153), Gracián provides an ingenious defense of the importance that the wise attach to appearances. Envious of his beauty, other birds have criticized the Peacock for his vanity and ostentation. Isn't it enough to *be* beautiful? How odious to flaunt it! Stung by that envy, the Peacock argues, with a touch of casuistry, that God Himself created light and saw that it was good, thereby giving His approval to ostentation. What sense would it make to create a rose or a diamond or a "feathered sun" like the Peacock if those qualities were invisible to others? So far, so good. But the Peacock has forgotten that it isn't enough to *be* beautiful, and *seem* so; you must also reckon with the envy of those who aren't. Listening to the Peacock and his detractors, the Vixen offers a stratagem:

when the Peacock raises his tail feathers, he will draw the gaze of the envious to . . . the ugliness of his feet. The gifted, says Gracián, ought to display some minor defect, commit some peccadillo, "toss Envy a bone," draw her "venom away from the heart" (page 54).

The same is true of all of the qualities. It is not enough to *be* wise or graceful or talented or even prodigiously gifted: one must learn how to "manage" that wisdom and talent, adapt it to the age in which one lives, show it off or conceal it, depending on the situation: excellence isn't right for every occasion, and there are times when best is worst and mediocre is safest. Gracián's lesson is *not* that things are not what they seem, but that things and people are both what they are *and* what they seem, and how they seem depends upon manner. Strictly speaking, the distinction is not between "appearances and reality" but between "inner" and "outer" reality: the one apprehended through the senses, and the other, only guessed at. The inner qualities—wisdom, courage, wit—must be combined with "outer" ones that can make them "shine": quickness, elegance, variety, grace, an agreeable manner, and a careful spontaneity. But even that principle is subject to modification. "Speak with the many, feel with the few": a maxim expounded both here and in *The Art of Worldly Wisdom* teaches us that there are occasions when it is best to play dumb, to row with the current, and to disappear into the crowd.

Was it really a priest who drafted these thoughts on simulation and dissimulation, these "new shortcuts to fame" and fortune?

Baltasar Gracián (1601–1658) was born in Belmonte, a village in Aragon, northeastern Spain. After studying at colleges in Zaragoza, Valencia, and elsewhere, he took his vows as a Jesuit (1634) and spent the rest of his life as a professor of theology and philosophy, preacher, confessor, chaplain, administrator, and writer.[4]

The times he lived in, and tried to adapt himself to, provided fertile ground for disillusionment. As late as the 1620s, Spain was the ruler of much of the New World, Europe, and parts of Asia. A mere half-century later, the empire had declined irretrievably, dragged down by war, internal strife, and economic problems. Those years of political misery coincided with a long period of cultural splendor: the Baroque. Gracián belonged to the age of the playwrights Calderón de la Barca and Lope de Vega, the poets Góngora and Quevedo, the painters Velázquez, Murillo, and Zurbarán; and, despite the restrictions placed on him as a priest, had the opportunity to relish much that was best in the arts. It was his good fortune to be assigned, early in his career, to Huesca, where he was befriended by Vincencio Juan de Lastanosa, a talented, wealthy nobleman, six years younger than he, whose palace Gracián describes admiringly as "the ne plus ultra of taste." In Lastanosa's circle of friends, which ranged from scholars to statesmen; in his inexhaustible library; in his collection of paintings, sculptures, weapons, armor, and coins; in his literary salon; and in his gardens, with plants from all parts of the world, Gracián found a microcosm of universal learning, a center of all human artifice, both intellectual and material. It was Lastanosa who paid for the publication of almost all of Gracián's books, defended his writings, and, surely, consoled and helped him in his struggles within the Jesuit Order.

Those difficulties began early and lasted until his death. They were caused not by the doctrinal contents of his works—there is nothing "unorthodox" about them—but by their worldly nature and by Gracián's stubborn refusal to submit them before publication to the approval of his Jesuit superiors. Dreading the frustration and delays of an official "imprimatur," and, probably, too proud to submit his works to the judgment of men less talented than he, Gracián published all but a few of them pseudonymously, bringing into the world, in the words of one of his superiors, "books which are hardly serious and hardly becoming to our profession."[5] In 1638, a year after the publication of his first book, *The Hero*, the general of the Society of Jesus was already writing, from Rome, to an Aragonese administrator, that it was necessary to move Father Gracián someplace else,

> because he is a cross to his superiors, the cause of unpleasant incidents which threaten the peace of the College, and because he has ill-advisedly taken it upon himself to bring up, and beg money for, a creature who is said to have been the son of one who left the Society; and, finally, because he has published a book [*The Hero*] under [the pseudonym of Lorenzo Gracián].

The publication of *El Discreto* (The Discreet) met with the same stern reaction, and in March 1658, a few months before Gracián's death, General Goswin Nickel issued a final, belated warning. For twenty years, Gracián had preferred literary glory to his vow of obedience as a priest.[6] In view of his continual disobedience, Nickel writes to one of Gracián's superiors, it will be a good idea to watch him, and from time to time inspect his hands and his room and his papers, and not permit him to keep anything under lock and key. And if Your Reverence should find some paper or other text against the Society or against its governance composed by Father Gracián, Your Reverence should lock him up and keep him locked up until he is humbled and recognizes his error . . . and not permit him, while he is in confinement, to have paper, pen or ink.

Gracián's friendship with Lastanosa and other influential aristocrats may have helped him smooth over some of these difficulties. Thanks to Lastanosa, perhaps, the Society permitted him to become the personal confessor of the Viceroy of Aragon, the Neapolitan Francesco Maria Carafa, and to accompany him to the court. The experience was not entirely to his liking. A letter to Lastanosa records his impressions of the capital and of the servants of the nobles with whom he has had to mingle:

I have no need for these people. Whether they need me, I don't know. I long to return to your collections. Here all is chicanery, lies, arrogance, vanity, for these people think there is no one in the world but them. As for me, I am *not* very humble and don't fawn on people, and so I leave them in peace.[7]

Not that Gracián lacked the style and substance to triumph in Madrid. He sometimes preached there to enormous crowds: an eyewitness reports that, on one occasion, four thousand people gathered in the streets hoping to hear him.[8] He must have found equally avid listeners in Valencia, a city he despised and ridiculed. His career there ran aground when he announced from the pulpit that he had correspondents in the underworld, and promised to read a letter delivered to him by the postmaster of hell.

Funny, subtle, obstinate, loyal to his friends, scornful of any sort of vulgarity, a lover of natural beauty, Gracián is far more delightful company than Jesuit records suggest. His superiors describe him variously, over the years, as *colericus* (irascible), *biliosus* (bad-tempered), and *melancolicus*. In years when he causes trouble—like the letter from hell—he is given poor marks for prudence (*prudentia mediocris; prudentia non multa*), but even then he is "fit for teaching and governing and for other sorts of ministry." At age forty-five, Gracián showed his versatility and proved his "sanguine" temperament as a chaplain in the royal army that rallied against French invaders at Lérida. In a letter to a friend, he recalls exhorting the Spanish troops, accompanying them under fire to the front line, attending to the injured, and administering extreme unction to the Spanish and their enemies. It was his own most heroic and harrowing moment: "They hailed me," he writes proudly, "as the Father of Victory."

The Hero, Gracián's first book, was published in 1637, when he was thirty-six years old. The first edition was dedicated to King Philip IV (the pallid, droopy Habsburg immortalized by Velázquez), perhaps in hopes of, well, royal largesse. Lastanosa, who had the book printed (like *El Discreto*) in a pretty, pocket-sized edition, tells us that Philip remarked, after reading it, "It is a little jewel of a book, and I can assure you it contains many great things!" Although the king assigned it "a prime place among the select books of his study"—Gracián himself spied a copy at the palace on a visit several years later—there was no other, more tangible sign of royal gratitude, and the dedication to Philip disappeared from the second edition. "Don't take payment in politeness" is one of the aphorisms of *The Art of Worldly Wisdom*.

In any event, *The Hero* brought Gracián his first renown, and his first problems, as a writer. By 1646 it had gone through four editions in Spanish, and had been translated into both French and Portuguese. More flattering still, a French Jesuit had plagiarized the book, retitling it *Le Héros François*, and the mutilated Hero was translated back into Spanish by a malevolent Catalan monk. It was a sign of things to come. For the next three centuries, Gracián's works would be imitated and translated into many of the world's major languages, from Hungarian to Latin to Japanese and Finnish. In France, Gracián was imitated by La Rochefoucauld, and in Germany his works were translated at least ten times in the seventeenth and eighteenth centuries. Two of his greatest admirers were the German philosophers Nietzsche and Schopenhauer.

The Hero, a response to Niccolò Machiavelli's *The Prince*, which Gracián dismissed jokingly as better suited to governing "a stable than a state," explores, in twenty-five brief chapters, the qualities needed to reach "heroism" in any occupation. Unlike *The Prince*, whose emphasis lies in the acquisition and preservation of political and military power, *The Hero* offers, in Gracián's words, "a politics for governing" oneself. Statecraft, he was to deal with elsewhere, in a little book entitled *El Político* (The Statesman, 1640), an enthusiastic homage to King Ferdinand of Castile. *El Discreto* (1646) continues along the same lines as *The Hero*, adding new qualities, drawing on a richer fund of experience, and transmitting it to the reader in a more varied and less succinct manner. The allegories, invectives, and dialogues in *El Discreto* and *The Art of Worldly Wisdom* (1641) prepared Gracián, and his readers, for his immortal masterpiece, *El Criticón* (The Critic, 1651, 1653, 1657), a vast allegorical novel of human existence—Schopenhauer thought it "one of the best books in the world"—in which two friends, wise Crítilo and naive Andrenio, make their way cautiously across the stage of life, from the springtime of childhood to the winter of old age.[9] Their circuitous route—through the *Great Desert of Hypocrisy*, into the *Cavern of Nothing*, or over the *Bridge of Buts*—brings all Spanish society, and much of Europe, within reach of Gracián's satirical pen. As in his other works, the element of chance is combined so strikingly with that of skill and calculation that life resembles a vast game of "chutes and ladders." There is no wise move without its hidden dangers; no fall that cannot lead to heroism. For every clever stratagem there is a counter-stratagem. Only change is constant: "Happiness lifts her foot, and sorrow crawls into her footstep" (page 95). Virtue alone guides us to the center of the game board, the Isle of Immortality.

The driving force behind all of Gracián's writings is wit in the service of moral acuity, and one of his most fascinating books, *Agudeza y arte de ingenio* (Wit calculated to force on us the conviction that absolutely nothing is worth all our activity, struggling and living, that all good things are vain and futile, that the world is ultimately bankrupt, that life is a business that does not cover the costs.[11]

The Spanish philosopher Miguel de Unamuno thought otherwise:

A pessimist? In the vulgar sense, the sense given to that term by cowards, by those who know nothing of tragedy—by the anti-tragic—yes, Gracián will seem a pessimist. But the man who could write "Ah, where can one go without having to fight?" was not a pessimist, no, no, he wasn't. And that is because what is worst—*lo pésimo*—is the peace of optimists, the peace of the peaceable. The peace of those who know war is something very, very different.[12]

Of the warfare of existence, few have written more poignantly and intensely than Gracián. And yet, for all his proud *desengaño*, one senses, in these pages, an intense admiration for human resourcefulness, a deep love of life, and a yearning for moral and artistic perfection. He wishes his readers "good cheer against

inconstant fortune, good health against the unyielding law, good art against imperfect nature, and a
good dose of understanding for all" (page 59). These
lines, reflecting both hope and disillusionment, could
serve as his epitaph (page 65):

> O life, you should never have begun.
> But since you did, you should never end!

Christopher Maurer
Vanderbilt University
Nashville

NOTES TO THE
INTRODUCTION

1. For a fine essay on *desengaño* in Gracián and other Baroque authors, see Otis H. Green, *Spain and the Western Tradition*, Vol. IV (Madison: University of Wisconsin Press, 1968), pp. 43–76.

2. Baltasar Gracián, *El Criticón*, ed. M. Romera-Navarro, Vol. II (Philadelphia/London: University of Pennsylvania Press/Oxford University Press, 1939), p. 25. The speaker is Argos.

3. See Jorge Checa's brilliant "Gracián y la lectura," *Hispanic Review* 59 (1991), p. 270.

4. The best modern biographies are still those of Miguel Batllori, *Gracián y el Barroco* (Roma: Edizioni di Storia e Letteratura, 1958), and E. Correa Calderón, *Baltasar Gracián. Su vida y su obra* (Madrid: Gredos, 1970). Studies of the life and works in English include A. F. G. Bell, *Baltasar Gracián* (Oxford: Hispanic Society of America, 1921), and Virginia Ramos Foster, *Baltasar Gracián* (New York: Twayne, 1975). For a lucid analysis of *El Héroe* and *El Discreto*, see Monroe Hafter, *Gracián and Perfection* (Cambridge: Harvard University Press, 1966); and of *The Art of Worldly Wisdom*, Jorge Checa (see note 3). The most convenient edition of Gracián's complete works is *Obras completas*, ed. Arturo del Hoyo (Madrid: Aguilar, 1960).

5. For documentation of Gracián's life as a Jesuit, see Batllori, *Gracián y el Barroco*, pp. 169–200. The passages quoted here and below are from pp. 174–75, 185, 194, and 196. Among the books that Gracián *did* publish with permission was *El Comulgatorio* (1655), a devotional tract translated into English by Mariana Monteiro as *Sanctuary Meditations for Priests and Frequent Communicants . . .* (London: Washbourne, 1875).

6. M. Romera-Navarro, "Reflexiones sobre los postreros días de Gracián," *Hispanic Review* IV, 2 (1936), p. 182.

7. For Gracián's correspondence, see *Obras completas*, pp. 1120–60.

8. *Obras completas*, p. xlviii.

9. *El Criticón* has yet to be fully translated into English. Part I was translated as *The Critick* by Paul Rycaut in 1681.

10. Anthony Grafton, "Dressed for Success," *The New Republic*, October 5, 1992.

11. Arthur Schopenhauer, *Manuscript Remains in Four Volumes*, Vol. IV, *The Manuscript Books of 1830–1852 and Last Manuscripts* (Oxford: Berg, 1985), p. 289. See also Vol. III, p. 348.

12. Quoted by M. García Blanco, "Gracián y las letras españolas contemporáneas," in *Homenaje a Gracián* (Zaragoza: Institución Fernando el Católico, 1958), p. 82.

TRANSLATOR'S NOTE

Three hundred years ago, one of Gracián's first English translators complained that "there is a vast number of more than ordinary fools, and mad men amongst us at present," and waved them away in a spirited preface:

> For the unintelligent and headstrong *Mobile*, that makes the greatest part of Mankind, they have nothing to doe with this Book . . . The Authour wrote not for them, well knowing that their inveterate folly is not to be cured but restrained; and that as it is very easie by force of words and long-winded Cant, to preach them out of their senses, so it is as impossible by short documents to sentence them into their Wits . . .*

The success of Gracián over the past few years, particularly in the United States, suggests that those words may have been too severe, and that new translations may find an ample audience. *A Pocket Mirror for*

---

* Anonymous, *The Courtiers Manual Oracle, Or, the Art of Prudence Written Originally in Spanish and Now Done into English* (London, 1685).

Heroes is a selection from *El Héroe* (1637) and *El Discreto* (1646). The section entitled "The Beveled Edge" draws mostly upon Gracián's allegorical novel *El Criticón* (1651, 1653, 1657), but also, occasionally, upon his treatise on wit, *Agudeza y arte de ingenio* (1648). In translating this book, I have consulted Saldkeld's *El Discreto, The Compleat Gentleman* (London, 1726) and Sir John Skeffington's *The Heroe* (London, 1652). I have followed the Spanish text given in Raquel Asun and Luys Santa Marina, eds., *El Héroe/El Discreto/Oráculo manual y arte de prudencia* (Barcelona, 1990), and in Miguel Romera-Navarro's edition of *El Criticón*, 3 vols. (Philadelphia/London, 1938–1940). Further information on *The Hero* came from Romera-Navarro's *Estudio del autógrafo de "El Héroe" graciano* (Madrid: *RFE*, Anejo XXXV, 1946).

Throughout the book, an ellipsis (. . .) indicates an omission from the original. The first-person pronoun in "The Beveled Edge" rarely refers to Gracián: those speaking are characters in *El Criticón*. Most of the titles in this book are mine. Criteria for selection were simple and not entirely arbitrary. I chose the passages I liked; those that seem most relevant to the late twentieth century; and those that worked best in English. I wish to thank Harriet Rubin, of Currency Doubleday, for having revived interest in Gracián; her assistant Jennifer Breheny for her good cheer and constant help; Bob Daniels for his thoughtful and meticulous copy-editing; and María Estrella Iglesias, to whom this work is dedicated.

C.M.

THE
HERO

TO THE READER

How singular I want you to be! With a book that is a dwarf, I want to make a giant. In the shortest of sayings, set down immortal deeds. I will try to make you the greatest person possible, a miracle of perfection, a king, if not by birth, by deeds.

Seneca formed a prudent person; Aesop, a shrewd one; Homer, a warrior; Aristotle, a philosopher; Tacitus, a statesman; and Castiglione, a courtier.

Copying some of the choicest parts of these great masters, I intend to sketch out a hero, a universal prodigy. That is why I made this pocket mirror: from the glass of others and my own fragile nature. At times it will delight you; at others, counsel and instruct. In it you will recognize the person you are or the one you ought to be.

You will find here a book neither of statecraft nor of economics, but a politics for governing yourself, a compass for sailing toward excellence, an art for reaching distinction with just a few rules of discretion.

I write in brief because your understanding is large. My words are as short as the subject is long. But let me not detain you: go forward.

HIDE YOUR DEPTHS

Let this be the first skill in the art of the well-advised: use your artifice to measure a situation. It is a great stratagem to allow yourself to be known but not comprehended; to bait expectations but never completely satisfy them; to let much promise more and the best actions create an appetite for even greater ones.

If you want to be revered, allow no one to take your depths. Rivers are awesome until someone finds a ford, and people are venerated until others discover the limits of their talents. Depths concealed cautiously will maintain your reputation.

Discovery is mastery; it allows victory to pass from one person to another. He who comprehends, commands, and he who conceals himself need never yield.

In certain games it is better not to reveal your strength on the first throw. You throw a little farther on each try, slowly advancing, and surprising your opponent.

It is worthy of an infinite being to make a bet large enough for the pool to seem infinite. This rule teaches us, if not to be infinite, at least to appear so.

Let us applaud the harsh paradox of the Greek

sage:* "The half is greater than the whole." For one half on display and the other in reserve are more than a whole that is fully within view.

One who showed supreme skill in this, as in all other stratagems, was Ferdinand, first king of the New World and last of Aragon, the ne plus ultra of her heroic monarchs.† He held his fellow kings in suspense more with his intellectual gifts, which shone more brightly each day, than with the new kingdoms he acquired.

And who was most impressed by this shining center of prudence? His consort and, after her, the seers at court: subtle in scanning his mind, sleepless from sounding his depths, eager to measure his worth.

How wisely he yielded to them and checked them! How cautiously kept them guessing!

O candidates for fame and for greatness, attend to this first stratagem for excellence. Let all know you and none sound your depths. Thanks to this stratagem, what is moderate will seem much, what is much will seem infinite, and what is infinite, much more.

---

* Pittacus of Mytilene (650–570 B.C.), one of the Seven Sages of Greece.
† Under the reign of Ferdinand of Aragon and Isabella of Castile, Spain conquered the New World.

6

CONCEAL YOUR
INTENTIONS

Art would be deficient if it merely taught you to conceal the limits of your talent. It must also teach you to disguise the impetus of your emotions . . .

If hidden reserves bring success, it is outright sovereignty to conceal your intentions and seal up your will. Show others the flaws in your willpower and your reputation will die a vulgar public death.

Your first effort should be to tame those defects; your second, to hide them. The first takes more courage; the second, more cunning.

If you give in to them, you sink from man to beast. If you bridle them, you keep up your credit, at least in appearance.

It suggests eminent talent to penetrate the will of others, and proves you superior to know how to hide your own.

Discovering someone's emotions is like opening a breach in the fortress of his talent. Political schemers pour through that opening, and often triumph. Discover someone's desires and you've found the entrances and exits of his will, and can come and go as you please, at any hour of the day.

Pagan antiquity made gods of people who had done fewer than half the deeds of Alexander the Great. They offered Alexander laurels, but withheld divinity. A conqueror of so much earth was unable to conquer a little patch of heaven. Why such scarcity amid such abundance?

Alexander darkened his illustrious deeds with the vulgarity of anger, and belied his triumphs by surrendering so often to emotion. What good was it to conquer a world if he lost the patrimony of a prince: reputation?

Excellence steers its course between the Scylla of anger and the Charybdis of desire. So let excellent people pay attention to mastering their passions, or at least cover them up so skillfully that no counter-stratagem can decipher their will.

This stratagem—concealing intentions—teaches people to understand and not be understood. It helps to hide their defects, deluding those that lie in ambush for the careless. It dazzles the lynxes that need the darkness of others to discover imperfection.

That Catholic Amazon, Isabella of Castile, who saw that Spain had nothing to envy from the queens of Egypt, was an oracle of these subtleties. When she gave birth she went into the darkest chamber in the palace, and with innate majesty sealed up her sighs in her royal bosom. She drew a veil of shadow across her face, concealing any expression of pain. How much more must she have scrupled in matters where her very reputation was at stake!

Cardinal Madruzzo* once said that a fool is not someone who aborts something foolish, but one who is unable to drown it.

Whoever can keep quiet can approach this stratagem. It begins as a natural inclination and, improved by art, becomes a godlike quality, at least in appearance.

A HERO'S GREATEST GIFT

Great parts are required for a great whole, and great qualities go into the design of a hero.

Passionate people give the first place to the understanding: origin of all greatness. And just as they cannot conceive of anyone great without a surplus of

---

* Cristoforo Madruzzo (1512–1578), governor of Milan under the Spanish king Philip II.

understanding, they know of no one who excels in understanding without being great.

The best part of the visible world is mankind, and within mankind, the understanding, and thus its triumphs are highest.

This capital gift adapts itself to two others—depth of judgment and elevation of the intellect—and a prodigy is formed whenever they come together . . .

The judgment is the throne of prudence, and the intellect is the sphere of wit. Which should be preferred, and in what proportion, is a matter best argued in the court of personal taste. I'm with the woman who prayed, "My son, may God give you the understanding of the good!"

Braveness, quickness, intellectual subtlety, and wit are like sun or lightning: a flash of divinity. Every hero has an excess of intellect.

The sayings of Alexander are the splendors of his deeds. Caesar was as quick in thought as he was in action . . .

Quick sallies of wit are as fruitful as those of the will are disastrous. They are wings for greatness, and by using them, many climbed out of the dust into brilliant sunshine.

The King of the Turks once deigned to appear on a balcony overlooking not the public square (the prison of majesty, the shackles of decorum) but a crowded garden. He began to read from a paper that the wind—either as a joke or to remind the king of its own sovereignty—snatched away and deposited in a tree. The king's pages, outdoing the wind and themselves, went scrambling down a ladder on wings of flattery. One of them—cup bearer of invention—took a shortcut through the air. He jumped, he flew, he retrieved and ascended while others were still descending. And he rose to unanticipated heights, for the king, charmed and flattered, rewarded him with an important position at court. For subtlety of spirit, though it has no realm of its own, can reign with someone else, and sharpness acts like the wild card of your gifts, combining with any of them, the very trumpet of fame. It can raise you the highest when your foundations are laid deepest.

Wit wears a crown in even the ordinary sayings of a king. The great treasures of monarchs have often perished, but their sayings are preserved in the jewel boxes of fame.

Words have sometimes conquered swords, and many champions were better served by a single witty saying than by the armor of entire squadrons.

The king of the wise and wisest of kings underwent his greatest trial, and spread his fame farthest, when he heard the case of the two harlots concern-

ing their child.* For justice, too, is accredited by subtlety.

Wit shines like the sun, even in the courts of bar-
barians, and Solomon's quickness was rivaled by that
of the Great Turk. As interest on a loan, a Jew proposed to cut an ounce of a Christian's flesh. Urging
his claim, he was as vehement before the Turk as he
was faithless toward God. The great judge commanded a pair of scales to be brought, and threatened him with death if he cut either more or less
than an ounce. He cut through the dispute like a
rapier and gave the world a miracle of quickness and
subtlety.

Quick-wittedness is an oracle in the greatest
doubts, a sphinx in enigmas, a thread of gold in the
labyrinth, and like a lion it often waits until it is in a
difficult situation to show its best.

But some people spend their wit as foolishly as
others do their fortunes. They shy from sublime
prey, like bastard hawks, but for paltry victims they
are eagles. They are mordant and satirical, and if
cruel wits are kneaded with blood, these are made
from venom. In them the laws of nature are con-
founded. For airy wit casts them down, burying them

---

* I Kings 3:16–28, where Solomon arrives at his famous solution of cutting the baby in two.

in an abyss of scorn, consigning them to the depths of common annoyance.

Until now, the favors of nature; henceforth, the excellence of art. Nature breeds subtlety; art nurtures it, sometimes with the salt of others, and at others by anticipated study and observation.

The witty sayings, the deeds of others, sow seeds of acuity in anyone with talent. The understanding makes them germinate, multiplying them into an abundance of quickness, a harvest of wit.

As for good judgment, it needs no defense and speaks for itself.

A KINGLY HEART

Philosophers have great heads; orators, great tongues; athletes, great breasts; soldiers, arms; couriers, feet; and porters, shoulders. Kings, great hearts. So says Plato, whose divine writings are cited by some in suits against intelligence.

What does it matter if understanding rushes forward but the heart holds back? Fancy conceives sweetly, and sometimes the heart finds those conceptions difficult to bring to light.

Subtle reasoning is often sterile, and grows weak when executed too delicately.

Great effects follow from a great cause, and portentous deeds from a prodigious heart. The sons of a giant heart are gigantic. It tackles deeds equal to its size, and seizes on matters of the first magnitude.

Huge was the heart of Alexander: just one of its corners easily held the entire world, leaving room for another six.

The greatest of all was that of Caesar, who found no middle ground between all or nothing.

The heart is the stomach of Fortune; it digests both of her extremes with the same ease and courage. A great belly has room for great morsels, is not unsettled by affectation, and does not grow sour with ingratitude. The surfeit of a dwarf is the hunger of a giant.

That miracle of valor, the Dauphin of France, who was later Charles VII, was notified that his father and the King of England had extorted a decision from the Parliament of Paris: Charles would not be allowed to succeed to the throne. Undaunted, he announced he would appeal. "To whom?" they asked. "To the greatness of my heart and the point of my sword." And so he did.

The almost eternal diamond does not shine as

proudly in the midst of devouring carbuncles as a stout heart in risks and dangers.

The Achilles of our time, Charles Emmanuel, Duke of Savoy, with only four of his men broke through four hundred enemy soldiers, and satisfied universal admiration by saying that, in moments of great danger, no company can compete with a great heart.

Excess of heart makes up for the lack of everything else: first to reach any difficulty, first to conquer.

The King of Arabia was once presented with a scimitar from Damascus: a rarity to please a warrior. His courtiers praised it highly, not out of politeness but with reason. Attentive to both courtesy and art, they went so far as to say it would be a "lightning bolt of steel" if it were just a little longer. The king sent for the prince, to ask his opinion, and well could he offer one, for he was Jacob Almanzor.* Considering it, he said that it was worth a city: an appraisal worthy of a prince. The king asked whether it lacked anything, and he answered that all was excess. "But, Prince, all of these gentlemen condemn it as too short." Laying his hand on his own sword, the prince

---

* Gracián seems to be referring to abu-Yūsuf Ya'qūb al-Manṣūr (d. 1199), conqueror of the Castilian king Alfonso VIII in the Battle of Alarcos.

15

said, "For a valiant man no sword is too short: when he takes a step forward, it grows long enough, and what it lacks in steel is supplied by courage."

Magnanimity shown before insults can crown this gift with laurels. It is the crest of nobility of great hearts. Hadrian* showed us a rare and excellent manner of conquering enemies when, standing over the worst of his, he said, "You seemed to have escaped . . ."

UNCOMMON TASTE

Real talent is never easy to please. Taste must be cultivated and improved no less than the intellect. When both are outstanding, they seem born from the same womb, twins of talent, coheirs of excellence.

A sublime intellect never bred lowly taste.

Some perfections are suns, others lights. The eagle makes love to the sun, and a winged little worm is lost in the light of a candle. To measure the depth of someone's talent, take the height of his taste.

---

* Roman emperor, born at Italica (near present-day Seville), who reigned A.D. 117–138.

To have good taste is much; to have elevated, much more. Taste is communicated from one person to another, and we are lucky to encounter anyone in whom it is outstanding.

Many consider it happiness (a sort of borrowed felicity) to possess and enjoy what they long for, and they consider everyone else unhappy. But those they believe unhappy think the same of them, so that one half of the world is always laughing at the other, and foolishness prevails.

It is a fine quality to have critical taste, a palate difficult to please. The bravest live in fear of it, and the surest perfections tremble.

Esteem is precious, and only the prudent know how to bargain for it. Be sparing with the coin of your applause and you will seem generous and rich. But squander your esteem and you deserve to be paid in scorn.

Ignorance is sometimes mistaken for admiration. The latter is born not so much from the perfection of objects as from the imperfection of our judgment. Perfections of the first magnitude are unique. So hold your applause!

One who had the taste of a king was Philip II, wisest of the Spanish Philips, who was so used to miraculous objects that he took pleasure only in what was a marvel of its kind.

A Portuguese merchant gave him a star of the earth (I mean an Oriental diamond): epitome of wealth, astonishment of splendor. And when all were awaiting Philip's admiration, or at least a sign of interest, they experienced only his disdain. This was not because the great monarch was unduly serious or rude, but because a taste like his, accustomed to miracles of art and nature, does not allow itself to be astonished so vulgarly. What a difficult moment for that fantastical merchant.

"Your majesty," he said, "I have abridged seventy thousand ducats into this worthy grandchild of the sun, and no one need be offended by it."

"What were you thinking of when you paid that much?" Philip asked.

"I was thinking, Sire," said the merchant, "that there was a Philip II in this world."

The king was more tickled by those words than by the preciousness of the stone, and gave orders to pay for the diamond and reward the man for his answer, showing the superiority of his taste both in the price and in the prize.

Some think that not to praise lavishly is to disparage. I would say that a surplus of praise implies a shortage of good judgment, and that the person who praises too much either mocks himself or mocks others. Why put the shoes of a giant on a pygmy? Measure first!

The world was full of the deeds of Don Fernando Álvarez de Toledo, Duke of Alba, and although he had conquered an entire world, his taste was only half satisfied. Asked why, he said that in forty years of victory, with all of Europe as his battlefield, and with all the best shields of his time as booty, none of it had meant anything; for he had never defeated an army of Turks where victory could truly be attributed to skill and not merely to chance or number; where the power subdued might have raised his experience and courage to new heights of esteem. It takes no less to satisfy the taste of a hero.

This stratagem—being sparing with your praise— should never turn you from a refined person into a godlike figure of mockery and mirth: that would be an unbearable disorder. It should make you an upright censor of whatever is most worthwhile. Some enslave their judgment to their will, perverting the offices of the sun and the night. Let each thing be esteemed for itself, and taste not be bribed.

Only great knowledge, assisted by great experience, is able to appraise perfection. And where the discreet person cannot cast his vote easily, let him not rush forward. Hold back, lest you reveal your own poverty when you praise the riches of others.

EMINENCE IN WHAT IS BEST

Only to the First Being is it given to embrace every sort of perfection. Because He does not receive it from others, his perfection knows no limits.

Some good qualities are bestowed on us by heaven; others are delegated to effort. To gain pre-eminence you need both. When heaven holds back with natural gifts, let diligence supply acquired ones. The former are daughters of favor; and these, of laudable effort. Often they are not the least noble.

Little is needed for individuals, but much for universal men: these are so rare that we can conceive of them, but they are usually denied to reality.

The singular can sometimes be plural; one person, many. To abridge into one thing or one person an entire category is the most intense sort of uniqueness.

Not all arts deserve esteem, nor all occupations.

To know everything is no grounds for criticism, but *practice* everything and your good name will suffer.

How different was Philip II of Spain from Philip of Macedon. The former—first in all, second only in name—chided his son for singing in his chamber. The other asked his son Alexander to run in the Olympic Games. One showed the scruples of prudence; the other stumbled in his greatness. Alexander was as hesitant to run as ready to answer: if his antagonists were kings, "Maybe, maybe."

Usually, what is most comfortable and enjoyable is least heroic.

A person who is truly excellent should not limit himself to one perfection or another, but rather, with infinite ambitions, aspire to a laudable universality. His knowledge should be more intense the more important his occupation.

It is not enough to know things superficially: a trivial matter. You will be criticized more often for being talkative than praised for being learned.

Some things are impossible, and to reach eminence in all matters is not the least of them. And not because ambition flags, but because diligence and even life itself give out. Practice makes perfect what one professes, and all the best things take time. But in undertaking something so long, we lose our taste for it.

A host of mediocre qualities cannot add a single carat of greatness, but a single eminence is more than enough to assure superiority.

There has never been a hero without eminence in one thing or another; it is in the very character of greatness. The greater the occupation, the louder the applause.

If one can win praise by kicking a ball of wind, what can one do with a sword, a pen, a staff, a scepter, a crown?

The Castilian Mars, on account of whom they say "Castile for captains and Aragon for kings,"* Don Diego Pérez de Vargas, whose deeds outnumbered his days, decided to end them in Jerez de la Frontera. *He* went into retirement, but not his fame, which traveled farther each day across the universal stage. Drawn by it, Alfonso,† a new king but an old appraiser of eminence, especially in arms and even among Castilians like Vargas, who were his rivals, went to look for him, in disguise, accompanied by only four of his men. For eminence is a magnet of the will, a bewitchment of affection.

The king reached Vargas' house in Jerez but did

---

* Spanish proverb much to the liking of Gracián, who was born and died in Aragon (northeastern Spain).

† Alfonso V of Aragon, "the Magnanimous" (1385–1458), warrior and king, ruler of Sicily and conqueror of Naples.

not find him at home. For Vargas, who was used to open battle, was beguiling his noble taste in the open air. The king, who had not objected to traveling from the court to a little town, did not mind going from there to the country. They spotted Vargas from afar, a hook in his hand, pruning his vines. Alfonso gave orders to halt, and told his men to hide. He alighted from his horse, and with majestic gallantry began to pick up the twigs that Vargas was carelessly cutting. Hearing a noise or, more probably, obeying an impulse of his faithful heart, Vargas turned round, recognized the king, and threw himself at his feet.

"Sire, what are you doing here?"

"Go on, Vargas," the king said. "I hope I am worthy to gather your twigs."

A triumph of eminence!

Let those who aspire to greatness do the same, assured that their work, their fatigue, will be repaid with celebrity.

The ancients were right to consecrate an ox to Hercules, showing mysteriously that praiseworthy work is a seedbed of good deeds, promising a harvest of fame, of applause, and of immortality.

THE EXCELLENCE
OF BEING FIRST

Many would have shone like the very Phoenix in their occupations if others had not preceded them. Being first is a great advantage; with eminence, twice as good. Deal the first hand and you will win the upper ground.

Those who follow are taken for imitators. No matter how much they sweat, they will never shed that burden.

Those who go first win fame by right of birth, and those who follow are like second sons, contenting themselves with meager portions.

The ancients, in love with novelty, not only esteemed but venerated the inventors of the arts. They turned esteem into reverence: a vulgar error, but one that shows the importance of being first.

What matters isn't being first in time, but being first in eminence.

Muchness discredits itself, even when it multiplies something excellent. But rarity makes even a moderate perfection more precious.

It is an uncommon skill to find a new path for

excellence, a modern route to celebrity. There are many roads to singularity, not all of them well traveled. The newest ones can be arduous, but they are often shortcuts to greatness.

Solomon opted wisely for pacifism, yielding warlike things to his father. By changing course he found it easier to become a hero.

Tiberius strove to achieve through the art of politics what Augustus did through his magnanimity.

And our great Philip II governed the entire world from the throne of his prudence, astonishing the ages. If his unconquered father was a model of energy, Philip was a paradigm of prudence.

This, too, was the way the radiant suns of the Church climbed to the zenith of their fame. Some owe fame to their holiness, others to wide learning, others to the magnificence of what they built, still others to giving new luster to the positions they held.

This sort of novelty has helped the well-advised win a place in the roll of the great.

Without leaving their own art, the ingenious leave the common path and take, even in professions gray with age, new steps toward eminence. Horace yielded epic poetry to Virgil, and Martial the lyric to Horace. Terence opted for comedy, Persius for satire, each hoping to be first in his genre. Bold fancy never succumbed to facile imitation.

A certain gallant painter* saw that Raphael, Titian, and others were impossible to overtake. Their fame grew even livelier after their death. He called on all his powers of invention. Rather than paint with refinement—for here he could only emulate them—he cultivated a certain bold, rough manner, gallantly telling his critics that he would rather be first in coarseness than second in delicacy.

Let this example spread to all the other professions, and the distinguished understand this stratagem: what is both eminent and novel will open an uncommon path to greatness.

A HEROIC OCCUPATION

Two cities produced two heroes: Thebes, Hercules and Rome, Cato. All the earth applauded Hercules, while Cato was an annoyance to Rome. One was admired by the entire world, the other shunned by his own city.

No doubt Cato was superior to Hercules: he ex-

---

* Probably Diego de Velázquez (1599–1660).

celled him in prudence. But Hercules conquered Cato in fame.

Cato's business was more arduous, for he tried to tame the monsters of public custom, and Hercules the ones of nature. But the Theban became better known.

The difference was that Hercules undertook praiseworthy deeds, and Cato hateful ones. Hercules' fame reached the end of the world and would have gone still farther if the planet were more spacious. As for Cato, the odiousness of his work enclosed him within the walls of Rome.

Despite all this, some people, including judicious ones, prefer an exacting, difficult matter to one likely to be applauded. They are more attracted by the admiration of a few than by the applause of the vulgar crowd. To them, deeds that win applause are "miracles of the ignorant."

Those who can perceive the arduous, exacting side of a superior matter are as few as they are eminent; their rarity is what gives that matter its value. Anything easy is perceived easily by all, and applause is common and cheap.

The intensity of a discerning few is preferable to the muchness of an entire nation.

And yet, it takes skill to find a praiseworthy occupation and prudence to bribe popular attention. After all, eminence is a public affair, and fame depends on universal suffrage. Matters that involve more people are more to be esteemed. In certain deeds, excellence can almost be touched, and because it is so evident, it is readily applauded. Exacting matters are like abstract thought: fame depends on interpretation and opinion.

What occupations are praiseworthy? Those carried out in everyone's sight, to everyone's satisfaction, but without doing harm to one's reputation. I would exclude those that are as empty of honor as they are full of show: an actor lives rich in applause and dies poor in reputation. To be eminent in something noble on the stage of *life*: that, certainly, is worthy of applause.

Among princes, only warriors enter the rolls of the famous; only they truly deserve the name of the great. They fill the world with applause, the centuries with fame, and books with their deeds, for war wins more applause than peace.

Among judges, the strictest and most just are those singled out by immortality, for justice without cruelty pleases people more than remiss mercy.

In matters of wit, too, there is room for applause. The sweetness of a good speech freshens the soul and flatters our ears, while the dryness of a metaphysical concept is a torture and an annoyance.

KNOW YOUR
HIGHEST GIFT

I don't know whether it is intelligence or luck that allows people to connect with their own highest gift, their king of talents.

In some the heart reigns, in others the head. Is there anything more foolish than to use courage to study and wit to fight?

Let the peacock be content with his feathers, the eagle with his flight. It would be grotesque for the ostrich to want to fly, risking an exemplary fall: let him pride himself on the strangeness of his plumage.

There is no one who could not have been eminent in some job, and yet they are so few that they are called rare, both because of their uniqueness and because of their excellence, and like the Phoenix they never emerge from doubt.

No one considers himself unskilled at even the highest occupation; beguiled by self-love, we are disabused only by time.

To be mediocre at an eminent job is a good excuse for not being eminent at a mediocre one. But there is no excuse for being mediocre in the lowest when you can be first in the highest.

A man spoke truth, though he was a poet, when he said, "Say nothing, do nothing against Minerva's will"* But nothing is harder than to shake people's belief in their own capacity.

Ah, if there were mirrors for the understanding as there are for the face! The understanding must be its own looking glass, but it is easily falsified and tarnished. As judges of ourselves we are quick to find escape clauses and take bribes from emotion.

Great is the variety of inclinations: nature multiplied them as wondrously as she did faces, voices, and temperaments.

There are as many tastes as employments. Even the least reputable and lowest of them have their ardent defenders. And what even the providence of a king would be powerless to achieve is made easy by inclination. If a monarch were to give out menial occupations—"You be a farmer, and you a sailor"— he would soon throw up his hands in despair. No one would be content even with the most honorable of them. But left to choose for themselves, people are blindly attracted to even the lowest.

Inclinations are so powerful that when they are

---

* Goddess of handicrafts, professions, and arts. The poet was Horace.

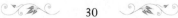

matched with the right job, they can do anything. But rarely do the two come together harmoniously.

Hernán Cortés could not have become the Spanish Alexander, the Caesar of the Indies, had he not shuffled occupations. As a man of letters he would have reached, at most, a vulgar mediocrity. As a warrior he climbed to the very summit of eminence, dividing the world with Alexander and Caesar.

So let the prudent beguile his taste, persuading it, without any sort of coercion, to get along with his particular talents. And once he has recognized his king of attributes, put it happily to work.

MEASURE YOUR LUCK

Fortune, as often named as little understood, is nothing else—to speak sensibly and, even, as a Catholic—than the great mother of Circumstance, the daughter of supreme Providence, never absent from her court, sometimes consenting and sometimes refusing.

She is a queen—sovereign, irresistible, inscrutable —smiling on some, severe to others, now a mother and now a stepmother, not out of emotion but for reasons forever veiled in mystery.

Masters of political discretion are always observing their fortune and that of their followers. If she has treated you like a mother, make use of her favor and commit yourself boldly: she is charmed when you take her into your confidence.

Caesar had taken the pulse of his fortune when, in a storm, he exclaimed to his exhausted boatman, "Stop being afraid! You are insulting the fortune of Caesar!" No anchor could have worked better. As long as the breath of fortune was blowing, contrary winds were not to be feared. What does wind matter if the sky is clear? Who cares if the sea is roaring when the stars are smiling?

Often people seem to undertake something rashly, but they are really subtle observers of their own fortune. Others could have struck a fine bargain with fame if only they had understood their luck. Even blind gamblers consult before tossing the dice.

It is a great gift to be fortunate; some say the greatest of all. Some prize an ounce of luck more than a pound of wisdom or a hundred of courage. Others base their reputation on bad luck and melancholy. The luck of fools: to find merit in misfortune!

A shrewd father uses gold to cover the ugliness of his daughter, and the Universal one gilds ugliness of spirit with good luck.

Galen wanted his doctor to be fortunate; Vegetius,* his captain; Aristotle, his king. A hero's patrons are courage and fortune: axis of all heroism.

But if Fortune has been a bitter stepmother, trim your sails and don't insist: her disfavor is heavier than lead.

The poet richest in maxims† will forgive me for stealing, and modifying, one: "Say nothing and do nothing unless Fortune is willing . . ."

Part of this political skill lies in discerning the fortunate from the unfortunate, so as to know when to compete and when to yield.

Suleiman‡ foresaw the good luck of our own Catholic Mars, Charles V, and was more afraid of his fortune than of all the troops of the West. He trimmed his sails in time and saved, if not his reputation (for he had already retreated from it), his life and his crown.

Not so Francis I of France, who chose to ignore his fortune and that of our Caesar, and was sentenced to prison for deliquency against prudence.§

Good luck and bad are contagious. So let the dis-

---

* Flavius Vegetius (fourth century A.D.) writer on the art of warfare admired by Gracián.

† Horace. See page 30.

‡ Suleiman I, "the Magnificent" (1494–1566), who allied with Francis I against Charles V.

§ He was imprisoned by Charles V, King of Spain and Holy Roman Emperor ("our Caesar"), at the Battle of Pavia (1525).

creet know what people to keep beside them, which cards to hold on to, and which to lay down.

KNOW WHEN
TO RETIRE

Anything in motion must wax and wane. Some speak of states of movement, but they are anything but static.

It takes great foresight to predict the decline of a restless, relentless wheel. The sharpest gamblers know when to quit: when prosperity is in play, misfortune is always for real.

It is better to sit down with honor than to stand by while fortune snatches away your winnings.

Fortune has much of femininity and little of constancy: so say those she has scalded. The Marquis of Marignano,* consoling Charles V at the Battle of Metz, told him that Fortune had not only the fickleness of a woman but the whims of a young flirt.

---

*Gian Giacomo de' Medici di Marignano (1495–1555), who fought for Charles V in Italy, Hungary, Germany, and the Low Countries. Charles's defeat at Metz occurred in 1552.

But I say that her changes are not fickle and feminine, but the alternatives of a just Providence.

The best refuge is an honorable retirement. A lovely retreat is as glorious as a brave attack.

And yet there are some so thirsty for luck that they cannot contain themselves once Fortune gives them a sip.

Here again, Charles V, firstborn of Fortune, provides a heroic example. This most glorious of emperors crowned his prowess with a prudent ending. He conquered the world with his fortune, and then conquered Fortune herself. For he knew when to retire, placing the seal of greatness on his deeds.*

Others went bankrupt in fame as punishment for greed. The happiest of beginnings have often led to the direst ends. Had they but used this stratagem, they would have secured their reputations.

A ring tossed into the ocean and restored in the jewel box of a fish announced the marriage of Polycrates to Fortune. But Mount Micalense, where Polycrates behaved rashly, was the tragic stage for their divorce.†

---

* Charles's abdication and retirement to the monastery of Yuste (1557) captured the European imagination.

† Afraid that his continual triumphs would make him odious to the gods, Polycrates, tyrant of Samos, threw his most valuable possession—a ring—into the ocean. A few days later a fisherman presented him with a fish, and the ring was inside. In 522 B.C. he was defeated in battle and crucified.

Belisarius went blind so that others could open their eyes, and the Moon of Spain fell into eclipse, giving light to many.*

No art can teach us to take the pulse of success: its heartbeat is defiantly irregular. And yet we can learn to read the signs of decline.

Sudden prosperity, where one success tramples upon another, is always suspect: for Fortune often steals in time what she offers in favor.

Success that has grown old often borders on weakness and senility, but extremes of misfortune often lead to a run of luck.

The Moor Abul, heir to the kingdom of Granada, was taken prisoner by his brother, the king. To distract himself from his misery, he sat down to a game of chess: good training for the game of fortune. A messenger arrived and told him to prepare himself to die (death always arrives by special delivery). Abul asked for a few more hours of life. That seemed too much to his jailer, but he gave him permission to finish the game. Abul played, and won his life and even the kingdom, for before the game was over another courier arrived with news of the king's death and an offer of the crown.

---

* The Roman general and the Spanish Conde de Luna (*luna* = moon), prime minister, whose sudden fall from power inspired many poets and moralists.

As many have risen from the scaffold to the crown as have fallen from the crown to the scaffold. The morsels of luck taste better with the bittersweet of things unforeseen.

Fortune is a pirate who waits until the ships have been loaded. A counterstratagem? Plan to take port!

WINNING FAVOR
FROM OTHERS

There is little point in winning the argument if you don't also win benevolence, taking the spoils of admiration and affection.

Many bring home applause and save their reputations, but not the goodwill of others.

This universal favor owes more to diligence than to the stars, though some say the opposite when they see that among those of equal merit, some are praised more highly.

The same thing one person uses to magnetize the will serves, in another, to repel it. The results depend on artifice.

To win the favor of others, it isn't enough to be

unusually talented, though that is a good start. It is easy to gain affection when you bribe people's understanding. Esteem summons affection.

The Duke of Guise,* famous in misfortune and rich in renown, understood the workings of this sort of popular favor, though he won little favor from his king, the third of the French Henrys. Fatal name for any monarch! In such lofty subjects, even their names are oracles.

One day Henry asked those around him, "What is it that Guise does, to bewitch people as he does?" He was answered by one whose sincerity would make him unique in times like ours: "Sire, he does good wholeheartedly: those who do not receive his good influence directly receive it by reflection. When deeds fail him, he resorts to words. There is no wedding he does not enliven, no baptism at which he is not godfather, no funeral he does not attend. He is courteous, humane, generous, the honorer of all and the detractor of none. In a word, he is a king by affection, just as Your Majesty is by law."

Happy popularity, or it *would* have been if the duke had coupled his own to that of the king. There was, after all, no need to compete. Though some say

---

* Henry of Lorraine, third Duke of Guise (1550–1588), was murdered by Henry III, who was envious of his popularity and suspected him of treason. The king himself (1551–1589) was assassinated by a fanatical monk.

 38

the opposite, the applause granted to an underling doesn't always make his master jealous.

The favor of the people, the king, and God are the three loveliest Graces that antiquity ever imagined. They hold hands and are closely intertwined, and if one must be lacking, let them go in order . . .

After Opinion, the prime movers in Favor's retinue are Courtesy and Generosity. With these two the emperor Titus came to be called "the darling of mankind."

A word of approval from a superior equals the deed of an equal, and an act of courtesy from a prince is better than a gift from someone else.

Forgetting his majesty for only a second, Alfonso the Magnanimous alighted from his horse to rescue a peasant. And that helped him breach the walls of Gaeta, which he had not even chipped during many days of bombardment. By capturing someone's heart, he captured a city.

The lowest of his critics say that his highest talent was common benevolence.

I would say that among the gifts that can bring us renown, this one has always been the happiest.

There is also the favor of historians, as much to be coveted as immortality itself, for their quills are the wings of fame. Unlike painters and sculptors, they portray not so much the wise acts of nature as those of the soul. Corvinus,* Phoenix of Hungary, used to say that the grandeur of a hero depends upon two things: doing good deeds and being generous to writers; for eternity is captured in characters of gold.

A CERTAIN GRACE

This certain, indefinable grace†—the soul of any gift, the life of any perfection, the brisk dispatch of deeds, the charm of words, and the bewitchment of all good taste—beguiles the intelligence and flees from explanation.

It is a mysterious formal beauty, the highest quality of any quality. The other gifts adorn nature, but this one adorns the gifts themselves: it is the most perfect part of perfection, a kind of transcendent beauty, a spell that is felt by all.

It consists in a certain dash and spirit, a jaunty elegance, both in saying and doing, and even in reasoning.

For the most part, it is innate, and it borrows little

---

* Matthias Corvinus (1443–1490), King of Hungary and a great patron of the arts.
† *Despejo,* in Spanish.

from observation. Until now it has never submitted to rules, being superior to any art.

Because it makes off with our taste, some call it ravishment; because imperceptible, others call it esprit; because quick, brio; because courageous, boldness; because spontaneous, ease. All this shows how hard it is to define, and how great is our desire to do so.

It would be insulting to confuse this grace with facility. It goes far beyond an easy manner, and is superior to flair and to style. Although it supposes a certain disencumbered ease, it adds the quality of perfection.

Actions have their Lucina,* and to this certain grace they owe their perfect birth; because of it they come fully to light.

Without it, even the slightest action is dead, and the greatest perfection unpleasant. It is something essential, not accidental; no mere ornament, but the foundation of the most important things in life. Being the soul of beauty, it is also the spirit of prudence; and being the breath of elegance, it is the very life of bravery.

In a leader it flourishes beside courage, and in a king, alongside prudence.

---

* Roman goddess of childbirth.

On the day of battle, intrepid grace is no less important than skill or bravery. It makes a general into a master of himself, and then of everything else . . . It is as spirited on horseback as it is majestic upon a throne, and even in a pulpit it can enliven speech and wit . . .

Who would doubt its usefulness in governance? Drawing on this certain grace, Alexander the Great, spiritual monarch of the globe, was heard to say, "Isn't there another world I can conquer?"

BORN TO RULE

This chapter covers a gift so subtle it would vanish into thin air were it not held fast by attentive curiosity.

In some people there shines an innate sense of leadership, a secret source of dominion that sparks obedience in others without need for orders and without the art of persuasion.

When Caesar was the captive of the island pirates, he was most their master. Conquered, he commanded; conquerors, they obeyed. He was captive only in ceremony, and master in the reality of his leadership.

People like these do more with a single stern look than others with all their diligence. Their words have a secret vigor, and they achieve more through sympathy than through brilliance.

The proudest minds and freest judgments bow to them without knowing why.

They are almost lions among people, sharing the lion's most important trait: dominion.

The lion is recognized by all the other animals with a kind of natural prescience: without ever testing his bravery, they foresee and flatter it.

Thus it is with these heroes, kings by nature: others advance them respect without asking for the collateral of talent.

This gift deserves a crown; if you also have understanding and a great heart, you lack nothing to become a political prime mover.

This lordly gift was enthroned in the Duke of Alba, a lord more by nature than by favor. He was great, and was born to be greater, and even his speech revealed this natural sense of command.

This quality is far from false gravity, from an affected tone of voice—the quintessence of what is abominable, though much less odious if it is natural.

It is further still from self-doubt, and the outright questioning of one's own worth, which is an open invitation to scorn.

It was a teaching of Cato, a sign of his severity, that we should respect, and even fear, ourselves.

Lose fear of yourself, grow too familiar, and you give license to others to do the same.

SUBLIME SYMPATHY

One of the gifts of a hero is to sympathize with other heroes. To sympathize with the sun is enough to make a plant gigantic and its flower the crown of the garden.

Sympathy is one of the prodigies nature has kept most secret. But its effects cause wonder and astonishment.

It lies in a sort of kinship of hearts, whereas antipathy is a divorce of wills.

Some people trace it to similarity of temperament, others to an alliance written in the stars.

Sympathy can work miracles and antipathy produce monsters. To sympathy we can attribute the wonders that common ignorance attributes to spells, and vulgarity to bewitchment.

Even the highest perfection is scorned by antipathy, and the rawest sort of ugliness is treated courteously by sympathy.

Sympathy and antipathy govern everything there is, exercising their jurisdiction over even parents and their children, trampling upon laws and laying aside privileges of nature and policy. A father's antipathy can take away a kingdom; his sympathy, bestow one.

Sympathy can persuade without eloquence, place a lien on whatever it wants, and serve warrants of natural harmony. It is the very character, the polestar, of the hero, but there are some with magnetic taste, who feel antipathy toward the diamond and sympathy toward iron. It is an aberration of nature to be attracted by dross and repelled by brilliance . . .

There are two sorts of sympathy, active and passive, and either is sublime when found in someone heroic. They are more precious than the great stone in Gyges' ring, stronger than the chains of Hercules.*

We are all attracted to the great, but rarely does one great person correlate with another. Sometimes the heart sighs or cries out without hearing an echo

---

*The ring that made Gyges, King of Lydia, invisible in his battles; the golden chains that allowed eloquent Hercules to hold his listeners.

of correspondence. Sympathy is the ABC, the very first lesson, in the school of desire.

So let the prudent take care to know and use passive sympathy. Let the attentive use this natural charm to repair or hide the defects of nature. It is unwise and useless to attempt anything at all without this natural favor. No will can be conquered without this weapon.

When found in a ruler, sympathy is the queen of all perfection, overflowing the bounds of prodigy. It is a column for the statue of immortality, rising from a foundation of favorable fortune.

Sometimes this great gift lies in lethargy, beyond the reach of the sweet breath of favor. Just as certain magnetic stones attract only the iron of their own region, sympathy is powerless outside its own active sphere. It depends on nearness, and never goes where it is not wanted.

So pay attention, you who aspire to be heroes. In the splendor of sympathy lies a new sort of dawn.

GREATNESS RENEWED

First efforts place talent in pledge, bringing worth and reputation into everyone's view.

Even a miracle of progress cannot give luster to ordinary beginnings, and efforts that come later are but a patch upon what came first.

A stylish beginning not only raises applause to a higher pitch, it dares talent to outdo itself.

Suspicion hovers around beginnings, eager to condemn. If once she enters, scorn will never leave.

Let the hero awaken with splendor, like the sun. The heroic must always attempt great deeds, with the greatest ones at the very beginning. An ordinary act cannot lead to extraordinary fame: if your job is a pygmy's, it cannot make you a giant.

Excellent beginnings are the insurance of reputation, and those of a hero must be a hundred times higher than the ends of a common man.

That sun of captains and general of heroes, the

heroic Count of Fuentes,* was born to applause like the sun, which rises huge and brilliant.

His first undertaking would have been the ne plus ultra of Mars. He was never a novice at fame, but professed immortality on his very first day. Ignoring the advice of many, he besieged Cambray, for his intelligence was as unique as his valor. He was sooner known as a hero than as a soldier.

Much is needed to disengage with honor from high expectations. Onlookers make the stakes even higher because it is so much easier to imagine a deed than to execute it.

An unexpected deed has always made a better impression than a prodigy expected by all.

A redwood grows faster in its first morning than does a lowly hyssop in five years. Robust beginnings point to gigantic endings.

Gigantic antecedents lead to extraordinary consequences: they affirm the power of fortune and the greatness of talent, and are attended by universal applause, by popular favor.

But energetic beginnings are not enough if progress is faint. Nero began with the applause of the Phoenix but reaped the scorn of the Basilisk. Join

---

* The soldier and statesman Pedro Enríquez de Acevedo de Toledo (1525–1610).

disproportionate extremes and you will have a monster.

It is no less difficult to advance your reputation than to establish it. Renown grows stale and praise turns as feeble as anything else, for the laws of time know no exception.

The philosophers said of the sun itself that it was old and ailing, and did not shine as brilliantly as before.

And so it is a clever trick both of the eagle and of the Phoenix to renew themselves in greatness, to freshen up their fame, and to be reborn to applause.

The sun finds new settings for its splendor, new stages for its brilliance, baiting admiration and desire with novelty or privation.

The Caesars lit up the world with their conquests, but returned each time to the rising sun of their Rome and were reborn to empire.

The king of metals, passing from the New World to the Old, went from an extremity of indifference to one of esteem.

Perfection stops shining when it happens every day. People grow annoyed with it and their appetite is sated.

EVERY GIFT
WITHOUT AFFECTATION

A hero must be clothed in every gift, every talent, every perfection, but must not be affected about any.

Affectation is the dead weight of greatness.

It consists in silent praise of oneself, and self-praise is the surest form of self-censure.

Perfection must belong to you, but praise belongs to others, and it is fit punishment, if you foolishly remember yourself, that the wise consign you to oblivion.

Esteem is free, is not fooled by artifice, and does not submit to violence. It yields more quickly to the eloquent silence of talent than to vane ostentation.

A little self-praise will rob you of much applause.

Those in the know take all affected gifts to be violent rather than natural, apparent rather than true; and reputation takes a dive.

Every Narcissus is a fool, and those in love with their own minds are incurable ones, for the illness lies where the remedy ought to be.

To display your gifts affectedly is foolishness, but

there is something even worse: to make a show of your defects.

Fleeing from affectation, some people fall head-long into it because they affect to have none.

Tiberius was proud of his powers of dissimulation, and never learned to dissimulate them. The loveliest aspect of any art lies in hiding it, and the greatest artifice is to cover it with a still higher one.

Twice great is the person who embraces all perfection but wastes no thought on his own. With a generous sort of carelessness, he awakens the interest of others. Blind to his own gifts, he makes others see like Argos.

This can be called a miracle of skill. Other skills open unique paths to greatness: this one seems to lead elsewhere, but guides us to the throne of fame, the canopy of immortality.

EMULATION

Most heroes had no children, or no heroic children, but many had imitators. As though heaven placed them here more to be models of courage than to propagate nature.

Eminent people are living textbooks of renown, and the learned ought to take down their lessons of greatness, repeat their deeds, construe their acts.

Think of the best and first in each category, not so much to imitate them as to emulate them; not to follow but to pull ahead.

It was Achilles who kept Alexander awake: sleeping on Achilles' grave awakened his desire for fame. The great Macedonian opened his eyes both to grief and to esteem, and cried not for dead Achilles but for himself, for he had not yet been born to the same renown.

Alexander was a challenge to Caesar, stinging him to the quick of his generous heart, making him surpass himself, until he cast Alexander's fame into controversy and made his own greatness a model for others. One made the East the glorious theater of his deeds; the other, the West.

And Alfonso the Magnanimous used to say that what the trumpet is to the thoroughbred, the clarion call of Caesar was to him.

So that one hero inherits from another; emulation leading to greatness, and greatness to fame.

In every occupation there is a first and a worst: miracles of excellence and their antipodes. Only the wise know how to appraise them, having studied every category of the heroic in the catalogue of fame.

Plutarch wrote the syllabus in his *Parallel Lives*, and, for the moderns, Paulus Jovius in his *Eulogies*.

The world is still lacking a true judgment and appraisal of heroes, but what writer would presume to supply one? It is easy to assign them a place in time, and very difficult in esteem . . .

CRITICAL PARADOX

Heroes are no longer punished with ostracism, as they were in ancient Athens. But the stinging criticism of Spain places them at risk.

Our critics would banish them immediately if they could. But they can do so only to the precincts of fame, the far-flung places of immortality.

Paradoxically, they are condemned for appearing faultless. A fine defense is to commit some venial sin, make some slip in prudence or valor, so as to entertain envy and bait malevolence.

These two are hard to escape, though one be a giant of splendor: they are harpies who, finding no vile prey, dare to attack the best.

There are people who secrete a certain metaphysical venom that can transform gifts, pervert perfections, and put the worst spin on the most justifiable of undertakings.

So let it be a political stratagem to sin a little, to toss Envy a bone, and deflect the venom of rivals.

Let Prudence inoculate herself, turning an ailment into health. She can set out some targets for rumor and draw its venom away from the heart.

Besides, the pranks of nature can be the crowning perfection of loveliness. A mole is also known as a beauty spot.

There are defects that aren't defects. Alcibiades affected them in valor, Ovid in intelligence, calling them "the sources of health." There is something of idleness in unruffled beauty: it leads to the sweetness of self-trust rather than to the polish of discretion.

What is the sun without an eclipse, the diamond without a cloud, the rose without its thorns?

Where nature is sufficient, art is unneeded. There is no need to affect new ones when your defects become you.

THE FINAL CROWN
OF HEROISM

All brilliance descends from on high. Virtue is the daughter of the light, with an inheritance of splendor. Sin is a monster aborted by blindness, with an inheritance of darkness.

Every hero has only as much happiness and greatness as virtue, for they run parallel, from birth to death . . .

O wise candidates to heroism, notice this most important stratagem, this best, most constant quality!

Greatness cannot be founded on sin, which is nothing; only on God, who is everything . . .

To be a hero in the world is little or nothing; to be one in heaven is much. To whose great monarch be the praise, the power, and the glory.

THE
BEVELED EDGE

ARTIFICE

Good cheer against inconstant fortune, good health against the unyielding law, good art against imperfect nature, and a good dose of understanding for all. Art is nature's complement, a second being that makes her more lovely and tries to exceed her in her works. She takes pride in having added another, artificial world to the first one, making up for nature's carelessness, perfecting her in everything. Without the help of artifice,* nature would be uncouth and unkempt. This, no doubt, was man's first job in paradise, when the Creator chose him His adjutant, electing him president of the world so that he would cultivate, perfect, and polish it. For artifice is the royal robe of nature. Adding brilliance to her simplicity, it always works miracles. And if artifice can turn a desert into a paradise, what can it not accomplish in the human spirit?

---

* Gracián uses "art" and "artifice" as near-synonyms here.

ART

She, too, is an enchantress. But whereas Circe changed men into pigs, Art changes beasts into people.

RETURN AND LOOK AGAIN

The privilege of the first man, and yours too! To take a fresh, attentive look at the greatness, beauty, harmony, strength, and variety of the whole great fabric of creation. Usually we feel no admiration because there is no novelty, and without admiration there is no attentiveness. We all enter the world with the eyes of the mind closed, and by the time we open them to knowledge, the custom of things—no matter how marvelous they are—leaves no room for wonder. The wise have always drawn on reflection, imagining themselves newly arrived in the world, pausing over its prodigies—for each thing *is* one—admiring perfection and ingeniously philosophizing. Just as someone strolling through the most delightful of gardens goes distractedly down its paths without noticing the loveliness of its plants or the variety of its flowers, and then, noticing, turns around and begins to delight, one by one, in each and every plant and flower, so it is with us: we travel from the cradle to the grave scarcely noticing the beauty and perfection of this universe. The wise always turn round, renewing their enjoyment and contemplating each thing with fresh attention, if not new sight.

FOUR WAYS TO KNOW

There are four ways to know much: live for many years; travel through many lands; read many good books (which is easiest); and converse with wise friends (which is most enjoyable).

ONLY ONE COMPLAINT

The great reader of a great book said that he had found only one defect: it was neither so brief that he could memorize it, nor so long that he would never finish it.

MAXIMS

The shorter they are, the deeper they are in wisdom. As when Epictetus reduced philosophy to two words: *Sustain, abstain!*

WIT

To perceive it makes one an eagle; to produce it, an angel. Delight of the cherubim; the raising up of man into an extravagant hierarchy.

Wit is one of the things that are better known in general terms than precisely. It lets us feel it, but not define it. In a matter this remote, any description is welcome. What beauty is for the eyes and harmony is for the ears, wit is for the intellect.

PARADOXES

. . . the monsters of truth.

CRUEL AND UNUSUAL

It is cruelty, and not art, to sentence the reader or listener to an entire hour in the company of a single boring metaphor: the ship of state, the highway of life, mountains to be climbed, whatever!

CANCEL THE DEDICATION

Those praised in a book take that praise, and more, as their due. What you meant as a gift is accepted as an obligation. In a second printing of one of his books, a writer listed the misprints in the first. Among them was the dedication.

AFFECTATION

There are people who would pay good money to be able to speak through the napes of their necks rather than through their mouths like everyone else. They would count it a sign of distinction.

NEW WAYS TO DIE

From a Castaway

O life, you should never have begun, but since you did, you should never end! There is nothing more sought after or fragile than you, and he who loses you once recovers you too late . . . Nature was a stepmother to man. Depriving him of knowledge at birth, she grants it to him at death. At birth, so that he will be insensible to the gift he is receiving; at death, so that he can better feel the mischiefs that conspire against him. O thousand times a tyrant the first human who, with scandalous boldness, entrusted his life to a fragile piece of wood and went shuttling over the inconstant waves! They say his breast was sheathed in steel, but I say in iron and error. In vain did Supreme Providence separate nations with mountains and seas, for man defiantly invented bridges for his malice. There is not a single invention he has not turned fatally against himself. Gunpowder, that terrible devourer of lives, is the instrument of his greatest ruin, and what is a ship but an anticipated coffin? Finding the land too narrow a theater for her actions, death devised a way for man to die in every element. We climb the gangplank of a ship as we climb to the scaffold: just punishment for our boldness. With reason Cato declared that the greatest of three idiocies was to embark.* O Fate, O Heaven, O Fortune! I could almost believe I am something when you persecute me so greatly. And once you have begun, you know no end but mine!

---

* The two others? To tell a secret to someone who cannot keep it, and to spend a complete day in idleness.

RUNNING WATER

People abandon their inclinations every seven years, and they change character even more often than that in each of their four ages. Man begins to live, or half live, perceiving nothing or little. In childhood, even the lowest of his powers lie dormant, the noble ones buried in an unfeeling puerility. He is as yet little less than a brute, growing like a plant, drawing nourishment like a flower. But in time the soul emerges from its swaddling clothes, fully exercises its powers, enters smiling youth, and becomes a sensual seeker of pleasure. Understanding nothing, man attends not to the intellect but only to his own temperament. And finally, always late, he awakens to the life of reason; and, recognizing himself a man, tries to be a person, esteems being esteemed, longs for courage, embraces virtue, enjoys friendship, searches for knowledge, and stores it up, attending to the highest occupations.

How right he was who compared human life to running water. Like it we glide away toward death. Childhood is a smiling brooklet that arises from fine sand, for the body is made of dust. And that brook wells up transparent and simple, laughs and murmurs, bubbles in the wind, puckers its face to cry, and girds up its length with the greenery of its banks. Youth comes forth in an impetuous torrent, races, leaps, throws itself down, colliding with stones, gliding over pebbles, thrashing at flowers, foaming, flowing more darkly and swelling with rage. Youth calms down into a river in maturity and goes slipping by, still and deep, its body hugely slow, all depth without noise. It swells, spacious and grave, fertilizes the fields, fortifies cities, enriches provinces, and is useful in every way. Man comes finally to rest in the ocean of gouty old age, abysm of ailments. There all rivers lose their strength and names and sweetness. By now he is a rotten vessel, taking on water in a hundred places, tossed about by the storms that pull him apart, until he is dashed painfully into the depths of a grave, on the shore of eternal oblivion.

THE BEST THIRD
OF LIFE

The body grows for twenty-five years, the heart for fifty, and the spirit always: a great argument for its immortality. The best third of life is the one that lies in the middle. People reach their perfection, and the soul comes into season. Thought grows substantial, talent keeps its promises, and opinion accommodates itself nicely to reason. At last, all is ripeness and prudence. At this point one should begin to live, but some never began life at all, and others start over each day. This is the queen of ages, if not absolutely perfect, with fewer imperfections than any other; not ignorant like childhood or crazy like youth or heavy and worn like old age. The sun shines brightest at noon. And Nature dresses her servants in different colors at the different times of life: blond and rose are the livery of childhood, and bright colors greet the sun of youth. In middle age she dresses the beard and hair in becoming black: a sign of deep reflection and prudent thoughts. She ends in white, when life is nearing its target, for the livery of old age is candor.

DUPED BY NATURE

Nature was crafty, and perhaps even dishonest, when she brought us into this world. She arranged for us to do so without knowledge and therefore without suspicion. For we come darkly, even blindly into this world, and begin to live without noticing that we are alive and without knowing what it is to live. As a child, man is hushed by any childish thing, content with any toy or trinket. He seems to have entered the realm of happiness, but is really a captive to fortune. By the time he opens the eyes of the soul, and realizes he has been tricked, he is hopelessly trapped, stuck in the mud from which he was formed. And what can he do except move forward in that mud and try to escape as best he can? I am persuaded that, were it not for Nature's universal ruse, no man or woman would want to enter a world so deceptive, and few would choose to go on living. For who would knowingly set foot in a false kingdom and true prison, only to suffer so many different punishments? In the body: hunger, thirst, cold, heat, weariness, nakedness, pain, and disease; in the mind:

deceit, persecution, envy, scorn, dishonor, turmoil, sadness, fear, anger, and despair. All this in order to be condemned, in the end, to a miserable death, with the loss of everything: house, estate, belongings, honors, friends, relatives, brothers, parents, and life itself just when we have come to love it most. Nature knew perfectly well what she was doing, and man accepted in ignorance. Whoever does not know you, O life, let him esteem you! But whoever has awakened to truth would choose rather to be transported from the cradle to the coffin, from the womb to the tomb. A common presage of misery is the tears we cry at birth . . . And the clarion call with which this man, this woman, this king or queen, enters the world is none other than weeping, a sign that our only realm is sorrow. What can we expect of a life that begins with the screams of the mother who gives it, and the weeping of the child who receives it?

KNOW THYSELF

The ancients wrote it forever, in letters of gold on the wall at Delphos, and in characters of esteem in the souls of the wise: "Know thyself!" Of all living creatures, only man mistakes his end, only he can stumble, led astray by the very nobility of his free will. And the person who begins by not knowing himself will never know anything well. What good is wisdom unless you are wise to yourself? We degenerate into the slaves of our slaves as often as we submit to vice. No robber, no sphinx, assails the traveler, assaults the living, like self-ignorance. Ignorance condemned to stupidity, when it does not know it does not know, and does not notice its lack of attention!

CLEAR AS WATER

Trust nothing completely, not even the clearest water; for its very transparency alters things, making them larger than they are and changing their shape, or hiding them in its depths, smiling and murmuring as any politician would.

TRUTH ON TRIAL

Alexander used to cover one ear as he listened to the prosecutor. "I'm saving the other one for the defense."

SO MANY, SO FEW

A huge crowd, few people.

DISILLUSIONMENT

I opened my eyes when there was nothing left to see. That is what always happens.

DRINK AND FORGET

As you climb toward the throne of Command, on the very first step of success, you will come to a strange fountain where people try to slake the thirst of ambition. One of that fountain's strange, contrary effects is that it makes us forget the past. I saw people drink from it and forget their former friends and acquaintances: witnesses to their former lowliness. They forgot even their brothers and sisters, and one drinker was such an arrogant barbarian that he did not recognize the father who engendered him, deleting from his memory all obligations, all favors received, wanting to be a creditor, not a debtor. Those who drank wanted to borrow, not to return. They forgot even themselves, and now that they were on the high seas, could barely remember that they had been spawned in puddles. They forgot all that could remind them of their dust and dung, all that would make them lower their feathers. They drank up ingratitude and affected gravity and remoteness, and wafted up strangely to their thrones, unable to recognize others, or recognize themselves. That is the way that honors change customs.

THE FACE OF MISCHIEF

See one lion and you've seen them all; one sheep, all sheep. But see one person and you've seen only one, and not even that one completely. All tigers are cruel; doves, innocent; yet every single person is different in character. A noble eagle will always breed noble offspring, but famous men do not breed famous sons; or small men, small. Each has his face and his taste, and none share an opinion. Clever Nature gave us different faces in order that each of us could be identified with his words and deeds, lest the good be confused with the ruinous, males with females, and the wiles of one be attributed to another. Many spend time studying the properties of herbs; how much more important it would be to study those of people, with whom we must live or die! And not all those we see are truly people, for there are fearful monsters in the gulfs and lochs of our great cities: wise men without works, old people without prudence, youths who disobey, women without shame, the rich without mercy, the poor without humility, lords without nobility, people who respect no laws, humans without humaneness, persons without substance, merit without reward.

NOTHING TO DO BUT GO FORWARD

Remarkable how man, a creature of reason, enslaves it to his bestial appetite. From this beginning, from this capital disorder, all of the other monstrosities are born, and all is thrown into reverse. Virtue is persecuted, vice applauded; truth falls silent, deceit speaks several languages; the wise have no books, the ignorant whole libraries; books have no doctors, doctors no books. The poor man's wisdom is folly, and the folly of the powerful is celebrated. Those who should give life take it. Youths drop their leaves, and the old blossom in winter. The upright are crooked, and man is too addled to tell right from left. He places good on the left, slings the most important things over his shoulder, tramples virtue underfoot, and instead of advancing, retreats.

How many would turn back if they could! There would be no one left in the world. We climb the ladder of life, and the rungs—the days—disappear one after another, the moment we move our feet. There is no way to climb down, nothing to do but go forward.

IN THE VANGUARD OF VICE

The vices got together, cracked a few beers, and declared man to be their common enemy, merely because he can reason. With the battle about to begin, Discord came into their midst, not out of hell, as some say, and not from a tent, but from the penthouse of hypocritical Ambition. True to his character, Discord started a quarrel about who would lead the assault. For each of the vices wanted to be in the vanguard. Gluttony argued she was first among sins: she won her first battles in the cradle. Lust described herself as the strongest and boldest of emotions, vaunted her innumerable victories, and was favored by many. Greed called herself the root of all evil, and Pride boasted of her lineage (she descended directly from heaven) and argued that she was the only vice worthy of men (the others were bestial). Anger butted heads with the whole pack, and they went at each other tooth and nail, helter-skelter, in total confusion. But Malice took the floor with a long and boring sermon: something about the vices linking themselves together, and never appearing alone . . .

"As for the honor of going first, who can doubt that it belongs to my oldest girl, Mentira,* authoress of all evil, source of all vice, mother of sin, snake with many heads, Proteus of many forms, centipede and master counterfeiter and progenitor of Deceit, that powerful king who rules both hemispheres, both deceived and deceivers, some out of ignorance and some out of malice. Let Falsehood and Deceit attack the unsuspecting innocence of man, in his childhood and youth, with their stratagems and schemes, ambushes and inventions, fictions, frauds, fallacies, and

---

* Spanish for "lie."

the rest of their huge Italian family. Let the other vices follow in order, and sooner or later, in childhood or youth, victory will be ours."

PASSPORT FOR THE VICES

That round antipode of heaven, that wanderer in space, that cage of wild beasts, that palace in the air, that hostel of iniquity, that house of all malice, that aged child—the World!—had come to such a state, and its inhabitants to such shameless madness, that they dared in public edicts to forbid all practice of virtue, under the stiffest of penalties. From now on, no one was to speak truth without being judged crazy; no one show any deference without being thought weak; no one study or know without being teased as "the philosopher" or "the stoic"; no one show any deliberation without being taken as dull and slow. And so on, throughout the virtues. As for the vices, they were given free rein, a passport good for the entire planet. The barbarous, lawless news went ringing round the world. But surprise! The virtues, which might have been expected to show extraordinary regret, did just the opposite, slapping one another on the back and showing indescribable delight. And the vices went wandering around dejectedly, unable to hide their sadness and chagrin.

A wise person wondered over this turn of events and consulted his beloved Wisdom.

"Don't be surprised," she said, "that we feel so content. Far from causing us harm, this vulgar lawlessness can only further our cause. It was no insult, but a blessing in disguise; nothing could do us more good. This time the vices will be destroyed; they do well to hide, and they're right to feel depressed. This is the day we will spread everywhere and make off with the world."

"On what do you base that prediction?"

"Simple. People feel a strange inclination toward what is forbidden. Prohibit something and they will die to get it. To make them look for something, you need only proscribe it. The greatest ugliness, when forbidden, is coveted more than the greatest beauty. Prohibit fasting and even Epicurus, even Heliogabalus,* will allow themselves to die of hunger, and if modesty were forbidden, Venus would leave Cyprus and join the vestal virgins. So cheer up! No more deception, no more disloyalty and ingratitude, bad

---

* The shamelessly profligate Roman emperor (205–222).

behavior, quarrels, or acts of betrayal . . . ! Theaters and casinos will close, all will be virtue, good times will return and people will use them wisely, women will be reconciled to their husbands and maids to their honor. Vassals will obey their kings, and kings will rule. Politicians will never lie, and there will be no gossip in small towns. Sex will salute the Sixth Commandment, and a new happiness will usher in the Age of Gold."

ENDS AND MEANS

One of the vulgar disorders of mankind is to make ends into means, and means into ends. What was meant to be something passing people make into something lasting, and they sit down to rest in the middle of the road. They begin where they should end, and end at the beginning. Wise Nature, in her foresight, introduced pleasure as a medium in all of life's operations, and as a relief from its most bothersome functions. She planned wisely, to ease us through whatever is painful. But here is where man comes undone. More brutish than any animal, degenerating from himself, he makes pleasure into an end and life into a means of getting there. He no longer eats to live, but lives to eat; does not rest in order to work, but skips work in order to sleep. Doesn't propagate the species, but only his lust. Doesn't study to know himself, but in order not to. Speaks not from necessity, but only to gossip. Doesn't enjoy his life, but lives for enjoyment. And thus all vices have made pleasure their chieftain. Pleasure: beadle of the appetite, forerunner of whimsy, quartermaster of the emotions, dragging people along behind him, tossing each one a scrap of what he most delights in.

SPEAK WITH
THE MANY

They say that Fortune was sitting on her burnished throne, beneath her sovereign canopy, more attended to by her courtesans than attentive to them, when two people came to solicit her favor.

The first begged her to make him fortunate among true people and favored by the wise and prudent. Those standing by looked at each other and said:

"Careful, or he'll run away with the world!"

But Fortune, with a grave, sad face, granted what he had asked for.

The second arrived and asked the opposite. He wanted to succeed among the ignorant and foolish. The courtesans laughed at such a strange and solemn request. Fortune smiled, and granted what he had asked for.

The two of them took leave, contented and thankful, forever wedded to their opinions. But the courtesans, who are always reading the face of their queen and scanning her emotions, had noticed that strange change of countenance. She noticed them noticing her and said brightly:

"Which of these two, my courtesans, do you think has been wisest? The first? Well, you are gravely mistaken. Know that he was a fool who had no idea what he was asking for and will never amount to anything. The second knew his business. He's the one who will run away with the world."

They marveled at her paradoxical answer, but she rescued them from their confusion:

"The wise are few. There aren't even four in a city. Four? There aren't even two in a kingdom! The ignorant are the many, fools are infinite, and the person who has them on his side will rule the entire world."

TRUTH APPLIES
HER MAKEUP

Truth was the lawful wife of Understanding, but Falsehood, her great rival, attempted to expel her from her bed and pull her from her throne. What ruses she invented! What slander! She began by calling Truth gross, unkempt, hard, and simple. And sold herself as courtly, smart, stylish, and gentle. And although she was naturally ugly, she was very good with makeup. She took Pleasure as her go-between, and before long had overthrown the noblest part of the mind.

Scorned and persecuted, Truth went to Wit to tell of her travails and inquire about a remedy. "Listen, my friend," said Wit, "in times like these, no food is more unpalatable than raw disillusionment; nothing more bitter than a mouthful of naked truth. Light that strikes the eyes directly can torture an eagle or a lynx. What do you expect from people whose vision is ill? This is why clever doctors of the mind invented the art of gilding truths, of sweetening disillusion. Take this down: you'll thank me for this advice.

You ought to be more of a politician. Dress the way Deceit does, borrow some of her jewelry, and I promise you success." Truth opened her eyes to artifice, and has never been the same. More inventive now, she devises stratagems, makes the distant appear close, speaks of the present in the past, ponders in one person what she wants to condemn in another, aims at Bill to bring down Jack, ravishes the emotions, counterfeits affection, draws on sweet and easy fables, and through ingenious meanderings like this one, comes to rest just where she wants to.

THE POOR

The philosophers say that nature abhors a vacuum, but in human affairs that aberration is produced each day. In our world nothing is given except to those who have most. Many are stripped of their possessions because they are poor, and see them given to others because they are wealthy. Presents are not wasted on the absent. Gold gilds silver, and one silver coin calls out to another. The rich inherit, and the poor have no relations. The hungry cannot find bread, and those with a full belly are taken out to dinner. He that has nothing shall have nothing. There is no equality in the world.

FOOLS

Who are they? All those who look like fools and half of those who don't.

MORAL ANATOMY

The divine philosopher was right to compare the human body to a resonant, living instrument. When it is well tuned, it makes marvelous music; and when it is not, it is all confusion and dissonance. It is composed of many, very different strings, incredibly hard to adjust to one another, and its pegs are always slipping. Some have called the tongue hardest to tune, and some the covetous hand. One person says the eyes, which never see enough vanity; another the ears, which cannot get their fill of flattery and gossip. Some say it is the fancy; some the insatiable appetite;

some the deep heart or bitter gut. But taking leave of them, I would say it is the belly, and so it is in all ages: in childhood because it is always hungry, in youth because of desire, in middle age because of its voracity, and in old age because of its craving for wine.

EARLIDS

We have eyelids but not earlids, for the ears are the portals of learning, and Nature wanted to keep them wide open. Not content with denying us this door, she also keeps us, alone among all listeners, from twitching our ears. Man alone holds them motionless, always on alert. She did not want us to lose a single second in cocking our ears and sharpening our hearing. The ears hold court at all hours, even when the soul retires to its chambers. In fact, it is then that those sentinels ought to be most wide awake. If not, who would warn of danger? When the mind goes lazily off to sleep, who else would rouse it? This is the difference between seeing and hearing. For the eyes seek out things deliberately, when and if they want, but things come spontaneously to the ears. Visible things tend to remain: if we don't look at them now, we can do so later; but most sounds pass by quickly, and we must grab that opportunity by the forelock. Our one tongue is twice enclosed, and our two ears are twice open, so that we can hear twice as much as we speak. I realize that half, perhaps more, of all things heard are unpleasant and even harmful, but for this there is a fine solution, which is to pretend not to hear, or to hear like a shopkeeper or a wise man. And there are things so devoid of reason that one walls up the ears with the hands. For if the hands help us to hear, they can also defend us from flattery. The snake knows a way to escape the charmer: he keeps one ear to the ground and plugs the other with his tail.

A WISE MOUTH . . .

How provident Nature was when she made the mouth not only for speech but also for taste! We can examine our words before we pronounce them, and sometimes chew on them, and see if they have substance, and if we notice they will embitter others, sweeten them up a bit. We can find out how a "no" tastes, and how someone will digest it, and coat it with sugar. Let the tongue be used to eat, and for much else besides, so that we can sometimes keep silent . . .

AND GOOD EARS

Nature formed our ears to be colanders of words, funnels of knowledge. She shaped the ear like a labyrinthine shell, with turns and whorls, or like the gratings and traverses of a fortress, so that words could be sifted, reasons purified, and so that there would be time to winnow truth from deceit.

THE PHYSIOLOGY OF DELAY

On a throne of tortoiseshell, in a slowly moving carriage, Delay was crossing the prairies of Time to the palace of Opportunity.

A creature of Maturity, she proceeded at a majestic pace, never hurrying or growing excited, reclining on two pillows given to her by Night: silent oracles of the best and calmest counsel. She had a venerable air, made beautiful by her many days; a serene, wide brow, more spacious because of her suffering; modest eyes accustomed to dissimulation; a large Roman nose, through which she let off the frenzy of anger and the flames of desire; a small mouth, like an urn holding treasure, not allowing even a sigh of pent-up emotion to escape (so as never to reveal the depths of her mind); a large bosom, where secrets could ripen and be held until their time; a stomach large enough for great morsels of fortune; a throat for anything life can offer; and above all, a heart like an ocean, to hold waves of passion and withstand the most furious of storms without roaring, without throwing off foam, without overrunning by even an

inch the limits of reason. In short, she was all greatness: great being, great depths, great capacity.

HAVING IT ALL

From a Conversation at the
Spanish Embassy in Rome

VITTORIO SIRI

On this chimerical mountain of pleasure, this fan-
tastic agglomeration of goods, as easily imagined as
difficult to obtain, what mortal ever reached the happiness he dreamt of? Croesus was rich but not wise;
Diogenes, wise but not rich. Who has ever had it all?
But suppose one does? The day he has nothing left to
desire he will be unhappy. And there are those whom
happiness makes unhappy. Some sigh because their
stomachs are full, and do badly because they are doing well. After making himself master of this world,
Alexander sighed for the imaginary ones he heard
about from a philosopher. I want my happiness to
come easier than that, and so I put on opinion inside
out and say the opposite of everybody else. Far from
thinking that happiness lies in having it all, I say that

it lies in having nothing, wanting nothing, and despising everything. This alone is happiness, and it comes especially easily to the discreet and wise. People who have the most things depend the most on them, and the person is least happy who needs most. After all, the sick need more than the healthy. The remedy for someone who craves water is not to add water but to remove the fever: and I say the same of the ambitious and the covetous. If you are happy with yourself, you can be sane and happy. What good is a cup if you can drink with your hand? Seneca said it well: if you can imprison your appetite between a piece of bread and a little water, you can be as happy as Jove. I cast my ballot like this: true happiness consists not in having it all but in desiring nothing.

VIRGILIO MALVEZZI

But wait. This sort of reasoning is more of a melancholy paradox than a sound piece of political advice. It would reduce noble human nature to nothingness. To want nothing and achieve nothing, what is this but to annihilate taste, nullify life, and reduce all to nought? Life is nothing but to enjoy the advantages of both nature and art, and to do so with measure and moderation. You do not make people perfect by depriving them of all good things; that would only destroy them completely. To what end are the perfections and pleasures? Why did the Supreme Maker give things such perfect variety and loveliness? What good are modesty and usefulness and good taste? If your reasoning had forbidden us what is dishonorable but allowed us all that is good, it might have passed as wisdom; but to place the good and the bad on the same level is simply a bold bit of whimsy. What I say . . . is that you can call yourself happy—or unhappy—if you think you are, no matter how many goods or evils surround you. It seems to me that the only true life is life with pleasure, and the only people who truly live are those who relish it. What use is it to have great happiness if you can't recognize it, but confuse it with misfortune? And on the contrary, even if people have nothing, that nothing is enough if they feel happy. In a word, life is pleasure, and the pleasurable life is true happiness.

CLAUDIO ACHILLINI

And yet, only fools are content with their own things. Self-satisfaction is the beatitude of the simple. "Lucky you," Michelangelo once said, "who are content with your vile doodlings while I get no satisfaction from anything I paint." I've always enjoyed a certain witty saying of Dante. Once, his great patron

Medici, wishing to find him, in disguise, in a crowd during Carnival, ordered those searching for him to ask everyone, "Who knows what good is?" Only one answered wisely: "He who knows what badness is." And they knew it was Dante. What a great saying! To know happiness, you must know its opposite. Only a hungry man relishes his food, and a thirsty one his drink, and a tired one his rest. Those who most treasure a prolonged peace are those who have gone through the misery of war. He who was poor best knows how to be rich; he who was jailed most enjoys freedom; the shipwrecked, a harbor; the exile, his country; and the unhappy, happiness. You will see many who do not relish their goods because they have never tasted evils. And thus I would say that the person who is happy is the one who has been un-happy.

AGOSTINO MASCARDI

So worth is want, bad goes first, and sorrow deals before pleasure? This would not be full happiness, but half happiness . . . And who would want hap-piness on those terms? I agree with those who say there is no happiness or unhappiness, fortune or mis-fortune, but only wisdom and folly, and that all hu-man happiness consists in being wise, and unhappi-ness in being foolish. The wise have no fear of

Fortune, they master her, and live above the stars, superior to any sort of dependency. Nothing can harm them as long as they do no harm to themselves. In a word: when people are brimming with wisdom, there is no room for unhappiness.

PIER GIOVANNI CAPRIATA

And yet whoever saw someone both wise and happy? Melancholy has always been the favorite food of the discreet. And you will see that the Spaniards, who are commonly thought the most deliberate and wise, are called by other nations the most gloomy and serious, while the French are thought happy, with all of their dancing and gaiety. Those whose minds reach furthest know evil most deeply, and know how far they are from being truly happy. The wise feel hardship more keenly, and since they are deeper, obstacles make more of an impression. One drop of bad luck can ruin their happiest moments. They are seldom fortunate, and their wide understanding works against them. And therefore, don't look for happiness on the face of the wise. You can look for mirth on the face of a fool.

AGOSTINO MASCARDI

In heaven, all is happiness; in hell, all is misery. In the world, midway between those two extremes, we

partake of both. Sorrows are shuffled with pleasures, and the bad takes turns with the good. Happiness lifts her foot, and sorrow crawls into her footstep. Good news follows bad. The moon waxes and wanes, lending its change to everything beneath it, and a stroke of luck follows a misfortune . . . The Preacher spoke of a time to laugh and a time to cry.* One day dawns cloudy, another clear, an ocean of milk or an ocean of bile. After an evil war comes a good peace. So that there are no moments of pure contentment, only watered-down ones, and that is the way we drink them. You need not tire yourselves searching for happiness in this life, which is a brief battle on the face of the earth. It isn't here, and this is the way it should be. For tell me, if life did not have so many sorrows, and if our lives were not besieged by misery, could people be pulled from her breast? If all were pleasure, comfort, and happiness, none would be willing to leave this vile nanny for the arms of their celestial mother.

---

* Gracián alludes to the biblical book of Ecclesiastes, "The Preacher."

VIRTUE

Man was made from the rest of creation. His perfections came to him as tribute, but on loan. Heaven gave him his soul, earth his body, fire his warmth, water his humors, air his breath, the stars his eyes, the sun his radiant face, fortune his possessions, fame his honors, time his ages, and the world his home. Friends gave him company; parents, character; and teachers, wisdom. And when he saw that all of these goods were movable, he is said to have asked:

"What, exactly, belongs to me? If all this is borrowed, what do I get to keep?"

"Virtue. It is yours alone, and no one can revoke it. All is nothing without her, and she is complete in herself. Other goods are in jest; she alone is in earnest. She is the soul of the soul, life of life, radiance of all gifts, crown of perfection, perfection of all being. She is the center of happiness, throne of honor, joy of life, satisfaction of the conscience, breath of the mind, source of contentment, font of happiness, and feast for the intellect, the will, and the memory. She is rare because she is difficult, and wherever she is, she is beautiful and well esteemed. All people want to resemble her, and few possess her in truth. The vices hide under her cloak and imitate her actions, and even the worst people want to be taken as good. All would like her for others, few for themselves. All want to be treated faithfully and not gossiped about, deceived, or insulted, but few bestow that treatment on others. She is lovely, noble, and gentle, and all the world conspires against her. True virtue has hidden herself away. When we think we've found her, we've seen only her shadow, which is hypocrisy. A kind person, a just one, a virtuous one, is as rare as the Phoenix, and no less immortal."

THE
BETTER PART
OF
DISCRETION

CHARACTER AND INTELLECT

They are the axis of radiant wisdom. Nature grants them by turns, and art can enhance them both. When character and intellect combine, they are stronger than Hercules and Atlas, and all of the other gifts shine too.

One without the other makes for only half a success, revealing the envy or the negligence of luck.

Intelligence has always won high praise, but to be successful it must be accompanied by the right character and inclination. And, to the contrary, a fine character makes intellectual defects more worthy of criticism.

Some wise people, far from vulgar in their taste, say that having a happy nature depends entirely on having the right sort of intellect, and they confirm it with etymology: for *genio* is said to derive from *ingenio*. But experience faithfully disabuses us, showing us monsters where these two are totally reversed.

These two qualities are the refinement and ornament of the soul. But the intellect is the crown of perfection. Man is a little world in himself, and the soul is his firmament. And what the sun is to the greater world, the intelligence is to the lesser. This is why Apollo was named god of discretion. Any advantage in knowing is an advantage in being. In the way we reason we are nothing less than more or less of a person.

Man's capacity makes him superior to animals, as angels are to men. His intellect is so superior that he presumes to partake of the divine essence.

If even one of our senses is lacking, it deprives us of much life, leaving the mind without its arms. How much more serious to lack a degree of imagination or of reasoning.

Sometimes there is as much difference between one person and another as between man and beast: if not in substance, then in circumstance; if not in vitality, then in personality.

One could exclaim of many what the fox said of the mask he found in a sculptor's workshop: "Ah, what a lovely head to have no brains! In you I find the vacuum so many philosophers thought impossible." Crafty anatomy: look at the inside of things. Outer beauty often gilds ugly ignorance. If he says nothing and wears a lion's skin, the simplest of beasts can fool the most astute. Silence heals foolishness. Not only does it hide what is missing, it turns it into mystery.

As for character, in a Time that was both lame and

blind,* it was glorified as divine spirit. The ancients called it "genius,"† exaggerating its importance. Those who erred only a little spoke of it as the intelligence that presides over the little world of man. And now that philosophy has become Christian, it speaks only of a superior inclination that promises good things.

Let character be singular but not anomalous; well seasoned but not paradoxical. Few people have a character that suits their condition: not all princes are heroic, not all scholars are prudent.

Good character is the fruit of a sublime nature and involves a ripeness of temperament that can lift up the very soul. It is what inclines us toward boldness or makes us choose occupations that can bring glory, and its powers of discernment cannot be exaggerated.

No one type of character or intellect is suited to every occupation: they do not always agree, either with each other or with the job.

Sometimes our self-love or sense of duty leads us astray, assigning the wrong occupation to each character. The person disgraced in his armor might have

---

* Chronos (Time) is often depicted as lame; he is blind here because he lived before Christianity.

† "Genius," or *daemon*: the protecting spirit that the gods assign to each person at birth, to accompany him through life and after death.

been wise in a toga. Chilon* gave this sound advice: "Know yourself and apply yourself."

Let the discreet begin to know by knowing themselves, attentive to their own temperament and reason . . . Doing violence to one's temperament has often led to disaster. It is a fatal torment to row against the currents of personal taste, intellect, and fortune.

Even countries and cities experience this pull and tug. Behavior often matters more than climate. Even Rome isn't suited to every sort of character and intelligence, and not everyone could enjoy learned Corinth. The same city is a home for one person and exile for another, and even our great Madrid, the mother of the world, from East to West, thanks to our great Philip, has been a stepmother to some. What happiness to find and recognize one's natural center! Crows do not nest among muses, the wise are not found in the din of the capital, and the prudent have little use for meddling courtesans.

In the variety of nations, too, we can study the sympathy and antipathy of characters and customs. It is impossible to combine with all of them. Who could bear the abominable pride of one, the detestable frivolity of another, the deceit of a third, the

---

* Chilon of Sparta (sixth century B.C.), one of the Seven Sages of Greece.

barbarism of another, unless our own origin permitted us to enjoy the qualities that seem violent to others?

It is a great stroke of luck to meet people of the same character and intellect; an art to know how to seek them; and a still greater art to keep them. There is no one who does not enjoy a moment of conversation, especially when one's character is singular. For the latitude of human nature is infinite, even between the poles of goodness and malice, sublimity and vulgarity, wisdom and ignorant whimsy.

It is bliss to have chosen our friends freely. Usually luck rushes ahead and determines where we will live, what we will do, and—even worse—assigns us friends, servants, and spouses, without bothering to consult with our temperament. This is why so many complain about her, as they languish in a sort of prison, dragging the bad qualities of others like a ball and chain behind them.

Judgment would be hard pressed to say whether it is better to lack character or a good intellect, and which it is better to have in excess. They can both be improved with effort, both enhanced by art. The highest happiness is to have them in the right proportion, in a heroic nature. Many have wasted that favor, deaf to their vocation.

AUTHORITY IN DEEDS
AND WORDS

Hesiod imagines that each of the gods gave us some useful quality. But it wasn't Pallas who gave us wisdom, or Venus beauty, or Mercury eloquence, or Mars bravery. It was art and careful, constant effort that added the perfections, one after another. And it wasn't Jupiter who gave humanity that majestic sense of authority in speech that we admire in some people; it was earned through constant practice.

Most people are extremists. Some have so little confidence in themselves, whether because they were born that way or because of the malice of others, that they think they can succeed at nothing. They insult their luck and their talent by not putting either to the test. Everywhere they find something to fear. They sooner find obstacles than advantages, and surrender so quickly to the muchness of their smallness that they attempt nothing on their own, and give others power of attorney over their actions and even their desires. These are the people who dare not dive into the water without a float, much air and little substance.

Others are full of themselves. Content with all they do, they feel no doubts and no regrets. They are wedded to their own judgments, and the more wrong they are, the more enamored they are of their reasoning, like children more loved for being ugly. Since they know nothing of caution, they know nothing of disappointment. Everything turns out well for them, or so they think. They live in bliss, and for a long time, as most fools do, for they have attained the untroubled joy of simplicity.

Between these two extremes of folly lies the golden mean of prudence, and it consists of a judicious sort of boldness, attended to by good luck.

I am not referring here to that sort of inborn superiority and natural lordliness I described in *The Hero*,* but to a prudent sort of boldness that neither cringes nor cavils, founded on a good understanding of things, or on the authority granted by age or social position: by virtue of any of these, one can speak and act with authority.

Even wealth can bestow it. Gold gives a special glow to foolishness, silver makes words tinkle and shine, and the braying of the rich is applauded,

---

* See pages 42–44.

 107

while the wise sayings of the poor are barely audible.

But the highest authority is that which rests on an adequate knowledge of things and long experience in different occupations. Master the subject matter and you will come and go with grace and ease and speak with the force of a teacher: for it is easy to master one's listeners if one first masters knowledge.

No sort of abstract speculation can give you this authority; only continual practice in one occupation or another. Mastery arises from an action done often and well.

Authority originates in nature and is perfected by art. Those who attain this quality find things already done for them. Superiority itself lends them ease and nothing holds them back: they shine, both in words and deeds, in every situation. Even mediocrity, helped out by authority, has a certain eminence, and a little showiness can make everything come out right.

People who lack authority come into a situation with misgivings. Once those doubts appear, brilliance is impossible. They breed fear and banish boldness, taking over the spirit, making speech and action seem dull. The spirit loses the sense of grace and ease one needs to be perfect.

Speak with authority and you will win the respect

and acceptance of even your most critical listeners. Authority will lend you words and even wisdom, just as fear will scare them away and freeze even a flood of eloquence.

When you tackle something with authority, whether in conversation or in reasoning, you win respect from the very outset. If you enter fearfully, you rush to condemn yourself even before others do.

It is true that the wise must pause, especially on unfamiliar ground, especially when they lack knowledge. When they suspect there are depths, they sound out the matter, as I will explain in *The Art of Worldly Wisdom.**

With princes, superiors, and all people in authority, tone down your boldness, but not so much that you reach the other extreme. What matters is moderation. You must try neither to annoy them with your self-confidence nor to allow your misgivings to make you lose face. Neither timidity nor rashness!

You should address certain people in a tone of superiority, not only when you are commanding them but even when you are asking or begging them for something. If these people see that they are held

---

* See *Worldly Wisdom*'s aphorism 78. Here, as on pages 132 and 141, Gracián refers to *Avisos del varón atento* (Advice to the Attentive Man), which was never published and appears to have become part of *The Art of Worldly Wisdom*.

in respect or fear, they puff up unbearably. These are usually the sort of people whom nature cast down and fortune has not quite managed to raise up. May God save us, above all, from those who make themselves young again in the corridors of power: insolent doorkeepers, hateful guardians of the law courts.

This supreme gift shines in any subject, more brightly in the highest. In an orator it does more than circumstance; in a lawyer it is essence; in an ambassador, splendor; in a leader, advantage; in a prince, an extreme.

Entire nations are majestic in nature, as others are shrewd and wide-awake. The Spaniard is lordly: what seems like arrogance to others is only an innate air of authority. Spanish gravity is born from temperament and not from affectation, and just as other nations go for flattery and obsequiousness, Spain applies herself to commanding others.

This sort of grandeur improves every human action, even the face, which is the throne of all composure, and even one's gait; for the heart is imprinted in one's footsteps, and the judicious use them to follow its trail . . .

Some were born with a universal sovereignty in all they say and do. It is as if nature had made them older brothers of everyone else. They were born to be superior, if not in their position, then at least in merit. They are suffused by a kingly spirit, and even their commonest actions set them apart as winners. They master others, seizing them by the heart, and there is room in their talent for anything. Others may be more knowledgeable, nobler, stronger, but the lordly air of these people makes them superior, if not by birthright, then by possession.

Others were formed from baser clay and more servile spirits, without an ounce of daring, trusting only the tastes of others, always questioning their own. Shadows born not for themselves but for others, who sometimes turn into vile flatterers and court fools. How often fortune gives a superior title to someone who would be talented as a slave!

This quality—authority—wears a crown and carries along other noble gifts in its retinue. It is followed by ease and grace, gallantry of action, a certain showiness, a love of praise . . . But be careful of the qualities that attach to it like grubs: affectation, rashness, arrogance, and the hateful habit of meddling. All of these qualities are the odious stepfathers of prudence and wisdom.

From: GALLANTRY
To: DISCRETION

The soul, too, has its boldness and style, much more distinctive than those of the body: a spirit of splendor whose acts of gallantry make the heart seem more graceful. The eyes of the soul are drawn to inner beauty, as those of the body to outer, and the inner wins more applause from wisdom than the outer does from good taste.

I am an uncommon gift . . . and only the magnanimous have room for me. Though a vulgar person is always changing heart, none is large enough for me.

My sphere of action is generosity, the crest of great hearts, and it is my business to speak and act well with my enemies: divine and faithful maxim supported by Christian teaching.

I shine most brightly at moments of vengeance. I do not do away with revenge, but improve it. I turn it into unheard-of generosity and enhance my reputation.

The French have always been gallant, and this was

the path that led Louis XII to immortality. Those who had insulted him when he was Duke of Orleans feared his succession to the throne. But he turned vengeance into gallantry with these inestimable words: "You have nothing to fear. The King of France does not avenge the injuries done to the Duke of Orleans . . ."

I make little of my victories over envy . . . and often keep them secret. I never pretend to have conquered, because I have nothing of pretension. And when I triumph through merit, I do my best to attribute it to luck . . .

At times I can make others feel indebted by giving up my due. When my decorum stoops to conquer, my reputation rises. I am notable when unnoticed and great when I am slighted, though I cannot always turn disdain into politeness: for there is no way to repair the cracks of slander.

It takes subtlety to turn a defect into a distinction, and I exchange the honors of effort and artifice for the insults of nature and fortune. Be first to confess your faults and you'll have the last word: this is not self-scorn but heroic boldness. Unlike what happens when we praise ourselves, self-criticism can make us seem nobler . . .

I usher people courteously out of tight situations, or compromising ones. I hand them the very word or

deed—a joke, a maxim, a deliberate slip, a paradox—
that can get them out of any pinch. It was I who
rescued Alfonso de Aguilar when King Ferdinand was
staying at his palace. The king complained that the
stairway was too narrow. "Your majesty," he answered, "I never dreamed I would have such a great
guest . . ."*

I am the beloved consort of ease and spontaneity.
Not only can I make any good action seem more
graceful, I can supply excuses for suspicious ones,
making them seem charming slips, the pardonable
results of boldness. I can make a king's caution seem
humane, a priest's timidity seem like courtly deference, and feminine scrupling, discretion. What others condemn as a slip in decorum, I dismiss as unwor-
thy of serious attention, but always with moderation,
so as not to fall into frivolity.

I have great enemies, so that my victories can be
more brilliant, and I trample on many vices on behalf
of many virtues. Only over the ruinous do I triumph
with any display, for there is nothing ruinous in me. I
hate any smallness, and have the largesse of noble
birth and a noble heart. My emblem is a hawk, the
most aristocratic of birds. I admire the hawk who

---

* I have borrowed this example from Gracián's *Agudeza y arte de ingenio* (see
Introduction, page xxi–xxii).

pardoned the little bird who warmed him through the night, or *would* have warmed him had his heart not been frozen in fear. But I also admire the little bird, who flew far away, so as not to meet with the hawk again and put his generosity to a second test.

The great have always been gallant, the gallant have always been heroes . . .

KNOWLEDGE

Hercules' prudence earned him more triumphs than his courage; and the glittering chains in his mouth, more applause than the fearful club in his hand. With the latter he tamed monsters, and with the former he bound the prudent, subjugating them to the sweet wonder of his eloquence. In a word, more surrendered to the discreet Theban than to the brave one.

Some people have a certain courtly knowledge: savory learning that can be conveyed in conversation and makes them well received everywhere, and sought out by the attentive and curious.

This is a manner of knowledge not taught by books or learned in the schools. It is studied on the stages of good taste and in the lecture halls of uncommon discretion.

There are some who relish wise sayings, are quick to observe any gallant action, and mindful of all that occurs in capitals and campaigns. They are the oracles of curiosity, the graduates of good taste.

Knowledge is passed from one of them to another in learned conversation, and punctual Tradition passes down these morsels to the knowers of the future like treasures of curiosity and wit.

In every age there are people of energy and spirit, and in ours there are probably no fewer than in the past. But the ancients got there first, co-opting authority and exciting the envy of the moderns. Presence is the enemy of fame. Anything prodigious, seen from nearby, topples from its reputation. Praise and scorn depend on time and place; the former comes from afar, the latter from nearby.

The best, most delightful part of this laudable learning is a knowledge of all that happens in the world, reaching the farthest courts, the remotest trading posts of fame: a practical knowledge of everything current, with an understanding of causes and effects; a close observation of the greatest actions of leaders, rare events, prodigies of nature, monstrosities of fortune.

It savors the mild fruits of study, examining what-

ever is ingenious in books, unusual in news, judicious in reasoning, and whatever stings in satires. It attends to the cleverness of one government and the blunders of another, and to the furor of war on land and sea, for war holds the world in suspense and provides fresh trials for reputation.

Its highest quality is a judicious understanding of people, a penetrating knowledge of the principal players in the tragicomedy of the universe. It defines each leader, applauds each hero. In each realm and province it discovers people eminent for their wisdom, courage, prudence, style, gallantry, intellect, and, above all, sanctity: stars of the first magnitude, the lordly splendor of republics. It assigns a place to each one, assaying his eminence and weighing his worth. It pries into the paradoxical qualities of one prince, the extravagance of another, the arrogance or vulgarity of a third, and uses this moral anatomy to form a concept of things and to balance the accounts of truth. This superior learning allows us to appreciate both words and deeds, heroic or courtly—the sayings of the wise, the malice of critics, the jokes of courtesans and politicians—and to draw moral learning from all . . .

As for conversation, this common science has sometimes been more useful, and brought more honor, than all the other liberal arts combined. It depends somewhat on talent, and when the heavens grant it, one has but little need of the other arts . . . Not that it shuns them; it takes them as its foundation. And just as courtesy stands out nicely against wealth, this kind of discretion falls like enamel on every other good quality. Conversation is the formal beauty of all the others, knowledge at its height, a display of brilliance, and it has sometimes been more useful to know how to write a good letter or say something witty than to have the law at your fingertips.

People who excel in this are rare: select treasurers of curiosity, traders in courtly erudition. If no one had troubled to observe and save the heroical sayings of Alexander and his father, of the Roman Caesars, of the Aragonese Alfonsos, of the Seven Sages, we would have lacked the greatest treasures of the understanding: true wealth for a superior life.

When you meet one of these rare, brave, wise spirits, savor the fruit of his learning. We search books hungrily for what is ingenious, but it is a still greater pleasure to meet the very oracles themselves. It is always self-interest that makes us seek out someone, but when we are attracted by agreeable knowledge or unusual attentiveness, that self-interest is far from vain. And don't begrudge yourself the taste of knowledge in order to deny someone else applause as a teacher.

Some come home from their travels as uncouth as they departed. If you go away without something to put it in, you cannot bring home a store of knowledge. Those of little depth make little use of worldly observation. But the discreet, like the ingenious bee, suck on the newsiest nectar, drawn from the loveliest flowers. Ambrosia was not made for the taste of fools, and no such knowledge is found in vulgar people, who never stir from the here and now.

Some place their happiness in their belly, asking nothing from life but food, while their higher powers slumber. Their reason is on vacation, their understanding languishes. Others find pleasure only in material objects, the lowest part of life, and are as indigent in understanding as wealthy in belongings. Only those who know live the life of people. Half of life is spent in conversation; and attentive learning, shared with others, is a feast for the prudent.

EQUAL YOURSELF

Defects gain nothing by mingling with the great. A spot on brocade looks even worse than one on burlap. And one of the faults and defects of the great is inconstancy. Some were born that way, others like to affect it.

This defect is like the ocean. Swaying back and forth, it praises and condemns by turns. It lifts someone to the stars, only to dash him, a second later, onto the rocks.

Novices are lost before such a stormy sea. But there are navigators at the palace whose experience allows them to laugh when others faint. They know that change, which torments us today, will smile favorably on us tomorrow. They look for the remedy in the very nature of the evil, which is vulgar inconstancy.

Ah, the prudent! How calmly they skirt the points and sound the gulfs! What do they care for the courtesies and the curtness of fortune? They are surprised by neither extreme.

Monstrous inconstancy obeys no reason. It is

strung together with a half-remembered "perhaps." It has no use for causes, merit, or circumstance (for adapting to things is always excusable and even prudent). The blank check of today's "yes" is the black look of tomorrow's "no." Today's relish is tomorrow's bitterness, with no good reason for either.

Fickleness is common in sovereigns: bound by no constraints, their taste can wander aimlessly. In the elderly it behaves like a child: they come to think that command is a matter of wanting or not wanting.

The wise have always been constant, not in their power, perhaps, but in their desires. Necessity can attack their strength but not their emotions, and before they bow to circumstance, they arrange things in their favor, and let it be known that change has arisen from necessity and not from whim.

Constancy helps us deal not only with people but with the virtues themselves. The inconstancy of Demetrius* was censored by many. Each day he was other than himself, and in war very different than in peace. As a warrior he was the capital of all virtue, and in peace the province of all vice. In war he made peace with goodness; in peace, made war on it. Such are the changes wrought by business and leisure.

---

* Demetrius I, King of Macedonia (336–283 B.C.), whom Gracián read about in Plutarch's *Parallel Lives*.

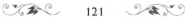

And what inconstancy was more monstrous than that of Nero? Instead of conquering himself, he fell down in unconditional surrender. Some compete with their better selves to reach their best (great victory of perfection!); others simply yield to their worst.

If change were always from bad to good, it would be good; if from good to better, better. But commonly it leads to worse, for we always see the face of evil and only the backside of good. Evil comes; good goes.

Some will say that all is inconstant in this fickle world, and that morals should follow nature. The earth itself is the more beautiful for the variety of its hills and valleys. What is more inconstant than Time, crowning himself with flowers or frost? The entire universe is variety in harmony, and if man is a little world in himself, why should it surprise us that he is a cipher of variety? Perhaps it is not ugliness but perfect proportion, drawn from unequal qualities?

Not so. There is no perfection in a wavering spirit: that would be inconsistent with the heavens. Nothing above the moon shows any change, and when it comes to wisdom, all ups and downs are ugly. To grow in good is radiance; to wax and wane, lunacy.

There are people so unequal, so different from

themselves on different occasions and on different matters, that they do amazing harm to their reputations. On some points they reason on wings; on others, perceive nothing, and never budge from their positions. One day all turns out well, the next badly, for even their understanding and luck are at odds. As for willpower, there is never an excuse for inconstancy; the crime is always intentional . . .

ALL SEASONS, ALL HOURS

For Vincencio Juan de Lastanosa

We mustn't always, my dear Lastanosa, be laughing with the smiling philosopher or crying with the weeping one.* The divine sage† divided times and assigned to each a purpose. Let there be a time for serious matters and a time for lighter, more human ones. A time for oneself and a time for others. For every action there is a season, and those times must not be disordered, or any of them singled out.

---

* Democritus and Heraclitus, respectively.
† A reference to Ecclesiastes.

We owe time to every occupation, and sometimes we hold on to it and sometimes let it pass.

The man of all hours is lord of all taste, the darling of discretion. Nature made us a compendium of the entire creation. Let art do the same for moral life. It is an unhappy person who is interested in one matter alone, even when it is unique or sublime. And what if it is a vulgar one, as most occupations are? The soldier speaks only of his campaigns, the businessman drones on about the deals he has made, the doctor about his patients, and their monotone makes others turn their attention elsewhere, or punish them with mockery.

Variety is always beautiful and pleasant, and here it is beguiling. There are some—most people, in fact —whom we turn to for a single thing, for they cannot do two. There are others with whom we cannot converse without touching on one particular theme: people of a single word, Sisyphuses of conversation, pushing their boulders up the slope of sweat and boredom. The discreet tremble before them, with good reason. Let one of these fools step on your patience and you'll find your good sense straining from every pore in your body, and you'll long for sterile solitude or for the age of gold within.

Abominable "dittos!" of some: hateful hammering on the skull of good taste. May God free us from such megamonsters of repetition, men of one manner, one matter!

Those who come to our rescue are friends of wide-ranging knowledge, compatible in character and intellect, always in season, ready for all occasions. One is worth many; a thousand of the others do not make one. We multiply them by the hour, in painful dependency.

This universality of will and of understanding is born of a spirit large enough for anything, infinite ambitions, and a palate for all. For it is no vulgar art to know how to enjoy things, and seize on anything good. A taste for gardens or, better, for buildings. Better still, painting, precious stones, the observation of antiquity, learning, and praiseworthy history. Best of all, a taste for moral wisdom. But all these are partial eminences, and those who are universal must combine them.

The discreet refuse to be tied to one occupation, or limit their enjoyment to one object, which is to confine it to unhappiness. Heaven made man without limits; let him fulfill that universality. Once heaven decided to serve food, it rained manna: a flavor that suits all palates, a symbol of universal taste.

Always speaking wittily causes weariness; always jokingly, scorn; always philosophically, sadness; and always satirically, unpleasantness.

The Great Captain,* a model of discretion, carried himself in the palace as though he had never crossed the battlefield, and on the battlefield as though he had never set foot in the court.

Another—not a great soldier but a great fool—invited a lady to dance and apologized for his clumsiness with a show of folly. He said that he had never learned to move his feet to music, only his arms on the battlefield. "Very well, sir," she answered. "In time of peace we'll put you back in your scabbard, or hang you like a harness in a closet, until you are needed."†

There is room in us for much knowledge, and pleasures need not interfere with one another. There is a time and a place for each.

Some keep no time but their own, and think only of their own convenience. But the wise keep an hour for themselves, and many for their well-chosen friends.

For everything there is a time, except for what is unseemly. I've often heard it said, my dear, learned Vincencio, that the life of each person is a play. The year begins with a Ram and ends with a Fish, and our

---

* Gonzalo Fernández de Córdoba (1453–1515), Spanish general and statesman, won the title of "the Great Captain" battling French forces in Naples.

† As often in his works, Gracián re-creates an anecdote from Baldassare Castiglione's *Book of the Courtier* (Book I).

lives have as much comedy as they do tragedy, as much fortune as misfortune. Each of us has to play all the parts, and do so on the right occasion. We play the wise man and the buffoon, the character who laughs and the one who cries. When our appearance is over, may there be relief and applause.

A WORD TO THE WISE

A Dialogue Between the Author and Dr. Juan Francisco Andrés*

DOCTOR: They say a word to the wise is sufficient.

AUTHOR: I would say that few words are always a challenge to the wise. And not only words, the face, which is the door of the soul and the index of the heart. Silence itself often gives us a hint, and says more to the wise than an abundance of speech to a fool.

DOCTOR: The truths that matter most are always half spoken.

---

* The Aragonese historian Juan Francisco Andrés de Uztarroz, who contributed an introductory note to the first edition of Gracián's *El Discreto*.

AUTHOR: But must be fully captured . . .

DOCTOR: These days, many disguise truth as foolishness.

AUTHOR: And many avoid it so as not to seem childish or foolish. Sincerity has fallen out of style. Only a few relics remain in the world, and they are discovered with mystery and veneration.

DOCTOR: When dealing with the powerful, we reveal truth little by little.

AUTHOR: And let them draw their own conclusions. Their survival or ruin depends on their ability to surmise.

DOCTOR: They say that the truth is a girl as modest as she is lovely; that is why she never appears without a veil.

AUTHOR: Let princes disrobe her gallantly. They must be diviners of truth, seers of disillusion. When others tell them the truth, they do so softly, and give it to them already chewed, so that it can be better digested and put to use. And the art of disillusionment—of giving someone the lie—has learned much from politics. It treads softly, as though at twilight, ready to retire to the shadows of flattery if it runs into a fool, or come out into the light of truth if it runs into wisdom.

DOCTOR: How moving it is to see the cautious compete with the prudent! Especially in matters of disillusionment. The first is all detention and hinting; the other, all attention and conjecture.

AUTHOR: Yes, for the intelligence must be adjusted to the matter at hand. In things that flatter us, we should hold it back from believing; in things that don't, give it free rein and dig in the spurs. For every step that flattery advances, wisdom takes a step backward. Reality is always less than half of what we imagine.

DOCTOR: Except in distasteful matters. In the slightest grimace, in the least little frown, the wise find new ground for reasoning.

AUTHOR: And sometimes grounds for embarrassment. It is hard to seize the much that is silenced in the little that is said. The wise handle prickly matters with special care. They approach slowly, with leaden steps, and—to dissemble—pass over the matter quickly, with a tongue lighter than a feather.

DOCTOR: When it comes to criticism or disillusionment, we are always slow to admit someone is alluding to us. We don't want to hear, much less believe. It doesn't take much to persuade us of what is good about us, but it sometimes takes the eloquence of Demosthenes to persuade us of what is bad.

AUTHOR: Besides, it is no longer enough to

understand. We must divine, for there are people who seal up the heart and allow their secrets and their feelings to ripen and even rot.

DOCTOR: Then do what the skillful physician did: take people's pulse from their breathing; the air in their mouths* can tell us their temperature.

AUTHOR: No knowledge ever harms us.

DOCTOR: But sometimes it brings sadness. And just as prudence thinks ahead to what others will say, shrewdness must take note of what they've said already. An insidious Sphinx lies in ambush along the road of life. Not to be intelligent is to perish. It is an enigma to know oneself. Only an Oedipus could solve that riddle, and even he needed auxiliary wits.

AUTHOR: There is nothing easier than to know others.

DOCTOR: Nor more difficult than to know oneself.

AUTHOR: There is no simpleton without malice—

DOCTOR: —and who doesn't see the faults of others twice as sharply as his own.

AUTHOR: He perceives the motes in the eyes of others—

DOCTOR: —and doesn't see the beam in his own.

AUTHOR: First step of knowledge: "Know thyself . . ."

---

* Words.

DOCTOR: A maxim sooner said than done.

AUTHOR: For giving that advice, Bias of Priene was numbered among the Seven Sages.

DOCTOR: And no one yet has become famous for following it! Some people know less of themselves the more they find out about others . . . They think much on what matters nothing, and nothing on what matters much.

AUTHOR: The fruit of idleness. Is there anything worse?

DOCTOR: Vain curiosity.

AUTHOR: "Alas, the woes of men, the vast, universal void!"*

DOCTOR: Returning to our subject, we should distinguish, also, between the restraint of one who speaks little and the wildness of one who speaks much. Some exaggerate, and some belittle. Let the attentive person learn to deal with both. As many have been fooled by disbelief as by belief.

AUTHOR: Which reminds me of what the Scythians taught young Alexander: that men are like rivers. Some receive what others discharge. The deepest are calmest and make the least noise.

DOCTOR: And there are matters where suspicion matters as much as truth. Caesar wanted his wife

---

* The author is quoting from the first satire of the Roman poet Persius.

to be above suspicion. Often, by the time we begin to feel suspicion, others are publicizing their conclusions.

AUTHOR: Words have more or less depth depending on the subject under discussion.

DOCTOR: Many have drowned by not testing their depths. Let the intelligent take soundings. And remember, the hardest part of swimming is keeping our clothes dry.

AUTHOR: Especially when they're royal robes. But enough of this. Let's return to our work: you to your *Ancient Zaragoza*, which is as full of learning as it is eagerly awaited, and me to my *Art of Worldly Wisdom*.

KNOW HOW
TO CHOOSE

Today all human knowledge amounts to knowing how to choose wisely. Little or nothing is invented, and, in what matters most, any novelty must be regarded as suspicious.

We are at the tail end of the centuries. Back in the Golden Age, they invented; later, added; and now all is repetition. All things have advanced; there is nothing left to do but choose. One lives by choosing, and chooses to live fully, and that gift is one of the most important nature can bestow. It is given to few so that it can be doubly precious.

Every day we see people of subtle mind and sharp judgment—studious, knowledgeable people—who are lost when it comes to making a choice. They always opt for the worst, are content with what makes least sense, enjoy what is least praiseworthy, while the judicious take critical note of them and everyone else shows scorn. They fail at everything, winning neither applause nor favor . . . Neither effort nor intelligence is enough when wise choice is lacking.

The importance of choice is transcendent. All occupations seek its approval, the greater ones more anxiously. It is the complement of any perfection, the origin and seal of success, and where choice is lacking, even when both materials and workmanship are excellent, all is doomed.

Without the gift of good taste, no one will ever be best in an occupation. This gift alone made many kings famous, as they ordered their affairs and selected their ministers. Others selected the wrong goals or the wrong instruments: fatal tarnish for brilliant scepters.

There are some occupations whose very essence lies in choosing; for example, all that involve teaching by delighting. Let the orator prefer the gravest, most laudable matters; the historian, sweet, useful ones. Let the philosopher marry elegance and pithy moral advice; and let all be attentive to the taste of everyone *else*, which is the norm for choosing, and which must sometimes be preferred to your own or that of someone else, even when they are excellent. Martial, the most delightful of our writers, said it well: "In a banquet I would rather please my guests than those seasoning the foods." What does it matter if the speaker satisfies his own taste and doesn't please his listeners? Who is it that is doing the tasting, anyway? *He* prefers subtlety, *they* a bold simile or metaphor, or the other way around.

In craftsmanship, too, there is room for taste. I have spoken elsewhere of two rival artists who competed for fame. One was so delicate and refined that each of his works was a masterpiece of its kind. And yet all of them put together could give no pleasure. The other was different: unable to bring even a single work to perfection. The latter won universal applause, thanks to his ability to select the right manner.

The power to choose arises from one's own taste, but how to know whether yours is good? Measure it against that of others. It would be better to use your own as a norm, and not depend on others, but this way you can be confident that what pleases you in them will also please them in you. From the ripeness of good taste comes good choice, and from there, success and happiness. If something succeeds in its absence, it will be mere chance.

Bad taste spoils everything, ruining even perfection by arranging it poorly. There are tastes so exotic that they always choose the worst, as though they had taken pains to err. They save the worst speech for the best occasion, and when expectations are highest, come out with the silliest words, wedding themselves to their foolishness.

How well a bee chooses, how badly a fly! In the same garden one sips on nectar, the other on dung.

Worst of all is someone whose taste is ailing, whether from ignorance or from whim; someone paralyzed in judgment who adds a second disorder, wanting to spread his illness to everyone and impose his paradoxical norms . . .

There are some whose taste is out of tune on some matters and in perfect pitch on others. But it is more common for those whose taste is rooted in nothing to produce no good fruit whatsoever.

Excellence in taste depends, also, on an adequate understanding of circumstance. It attends to the occasion: first rule for success. It sees beyond inherent excellence and devotes some thought to fittingness, for sometimes the best is worst for the occasion. When excellence shakes hands with occasion, success ensues. Taste is governed by time, attends to social position, distinguishes carefully between one person and another, and adjusts itself to the occasion. Only then can selection be perfect.

Emotion is the declared enemy of prudence and thus of wise selection. It cares nothing for what is fitting, only for its effect, and it would rather indulge its whims than hit the mark. It makes no distinction between "best" and "favorite": voluntary self-deception.

The matters governed by choice are many, and some are sublime. We choose our occupation and condition in life, and the effects of that choice last a lifetime. We get it forever right or wrong, and sometimes bear the burden of irremediable failure. It is a shame that the most important resolutions are taken in early youth, when we are all but destitute of knowledge and experience and when even the greatest prudence and ripest maturity would hardly be enough.

It is no less important to select friends wisely: friendship should reflect choice, not chance. Relatives, too, should be carefully selected: helpers in life, but often useless enemies.

If one could choose one's children, it would be the greatest of blessings. And yet there is so much whimsy in the world that people would probably select the worst. Perhaps nature did us a favor by removing that choice, for even those who were given good children have often made them bad through example or neglect. For there are many who waste nature's favors and those of fortune.

There is no perfection where there is no selection. And that gift is really two: liberty to choose and the art of choosing wisely. To lack it is to play blindman's buff with chance. If you do not choose wisely, follow the advice or the example of those who do.

MAKE YOURSELF SCARCE

Excellence is no sooner used than abused. All covet something excellent and thereby make it common. Once it loses its reputation for rarity, it is

scorned as vulgar; and sadly, its very excellence is the cause of its ruin. Universal applause turns into universal annoyance.

Abundance is the termite that nibbles at all sorts of excellent things. Born from their fame, feeding on their continual display, it can topple and walk on the highest greatness. Continual display turns anything into vulgarity.

It is a great defect to be good for nothing, but just as bad to be good for everything, or want to be so. There are people whose many gifts make them sought by all: all matters are submitted to their direction or management, even those that do not agree with their character and training. Success seems certain in all they put their hand to. Their very excellence, and the laziness of others, parade them constantly through the public view. Their very reputation turns them into involuntary meddlers. But this is less a defect than a result of circumstance: their surplus talent wears them down; they are lost because they are found so often. How wise it is to cultivate the golden mean! But how few know how to make themselves a little scarcer!

Fine paintings and precious tapestries pay a tax on their greatness: they are taken out on every public-occasion, and with people rubbing continually against them, they quickly become useless or (what is worse) common.

Some people, neither few nor wise, are friends of all who come calling. They sleep not, eat not, rest not. Any business is a boon to them; their best day, their busiest. They come before they're called, and inject themselves into everything. Adding rashness to their meddling—the fur lining of foolishness—they undertake great deeds. All that others notice is their hair, or their necktie, which, at least, ties their tongues for gossip and murmuring, and keeps their malice from being taken seriously.

I don't know which is more annoying: to run into these people so often or to hear them mentioned at all hours of the day and night. They begin by being popular and end up being hateful.

Not everything leaves their hands with the same success. Sometimes what was going to be a noble deed slips from the potter's wheel (or the wheel of fortune) and smashes their reputation. In the rush to please everyone, which is impossible, they end up pleasing no one at all, which is easy.

Those seen too often are envied or detested; for publicity leads to rivalry. Their eminence is merely an obstacle: everyone trips on the brick that stands out. A reputation is as easily broken as glass. Keep it in retirement, in the bubble wrap of humility.

Some want to be the roosters of publicity; the more they sing, the more they annoy. One or two shrieks would be enough to advise or awaken. No one asks the cock or the crow for an encore.

The most delicious food is less delightful on the second tasting; and on the third, if it is too soon, we are already weary of it. It would be better to offer only the first fruits of taste and create an appetite for more. If this is true of bodily food, what of the delights of the understanding? The greater the taster, the more demanding. Excellence is worth more when rare; what seems most difficult is most highly esteemed.

Excellence is as coveted, reputation as brilliant, as they are retiring. Any moderation is healthy; in public appearance, it conserves life and fame. The same applies to beauty. Show it off on all occasions, combine it with anything, like a wild card, and your reward will be indifference and, eventually, scorn.

One woman who knew of this vulgar risk, and who knew how to make the most of the most beauty, was Nero's famous wife, Poppaea. She managed her appearance so skillfully, turning over her cards slowly, one by one, that she made even herself envious. One day she veiled her eyes and forehead—

another, her mouth and cheeks—without ever showing the royal flush of her beauty. But people knew it was there, and with this she won greater fame.

A great lesson, and one that I will deal with in *The Art of Worldly Wisdom*: to know how to win esteem, how to sell one's excellence, covering it in order to conserve it, and even increase it with desire.*

A good confirmation of this maxim is provided by an emerald merchant from the New World. He brought many of them, and they were all of high quality. He exposed the first to the expertise of a jeweler, who paid him in admiration. He took out the second, superior in every way, expecting more appreciation; but the jeweler halved his esteem. He devalued the third and fourth in the same proportion, so that every stone was more precious but less prized. The owner was amazed at such a calculus, and heard the cause, which we, too, can learn from: when something is precious, abundance does it harm; where rarity is ruined, so, too, is esteem.

Ah, prudent people: if you want to win immortal fame, don't be a wild card. Be perfect in the extreme, but in matters of publicity, keep to the golden mean.

---

* See aphorism 150 in *The Art of Worldly Wisdom*.

THE DREGS OF
APPLAUSE

If I believed in Fortune, as the vulgar do, I would imagine her house to have two doors, one very different from the other. One would be made of pebbles fit for an alabaster urn, and the other of dark ones foretelling unhappiness.* At one door would be Content, Rest, Honor, Fulfillment, Wealth, and all manner of Success; at the other, Sadness, Toil, Hunger, Scorn, Poverty: the whole sorry family of Misfortune. All mortals frequent this house and pass through one of those doors. But it is an inviolable law, enforced with great strictness, that if you enter through one you must leave through the other. Those who enter through Pleasure must depart through Sorrow, and vice versa.

It is the common humiliation of the fortunate to make happy entrances and tragic exits. The applause they hear at the beginning makes for noisier mumbling at the end. What matters isn't the popular ac-

---

* Allusion to the ancient custom of marking good days with white pebbles, bad days with dark ones.

142

claim of an entrance, for that is very common, but the general regret of an exit, for that is exceedingly rare . . .

Every position has a showy facade and a very humble backyard. We are hailed as conquerors when we take up some important position, but often cursed when we leave. We get warm applause at the beginning, because vulgar people like change or because they hope for personal favors and advancement. But how quiet the end is . . . ! Fortune is as courteous to those coming as she is rude to those going . . . The clothes she wears are showy in the extreme: she wears white on her breast and black on her shoulders. Not to wait for her dark side is to see the light. The beginning of prudence is a prudent ending . . . The wise pilot steers his ship not at the bow but at the helm. Let us do the same on the voyage of life . . .

A certain Roman* gave a great rule for beginnings and endings when he said that he had achieved all dignities and honors before he wanted them, and had left them all before *others* did. The latter matters most, though both matter greatly. For beginnings have something of chance in them, but endings require a singular act of prudence. Misfortune is often

---

* Pompey.

the punishment for staying too long, and it is a great glory to anticipate it. The wise console themselves by deserting their privileges before they are deserted by them, and are doubly wise for that foresight. They regulate and manage their own success, guiding it toward a fine ending, conserving people's favor so that they will be as missed when they depart as they were welcome when they arrived.

Nothing should be ended by breaking it off suddenly and completely, whether friendship, favor, or employment. For any rupture harms our reputation and causes pain.

Few lucky people have escaped the final reverses of Fortune. Great luck has bitter dregs and leaves a bitter aftertaste. Some are saved by chance, others by their own prudence. Some, heroes, had endings scripted by heaven! Moses disappeared and was mysteriously glorified, and Elijah was swept up in a whirlwind that turned his end into a triumph. Even in pagan antiquity, certain endings caused doubt and wonder. The end of Romulus turned senatorial malice into mystery and made him more greatly venerated.*

Others, though eminently heroic, tarnished the

---

* The legendary founder of Rome was slain, but his assassins told the populace he had been struck by lightning, and turned him into a God.

glory of their deeds with the lowliness of their endings. When Hercules turned to knitting,* he cut the thread of his own fame, saddening the brave and instructing the wise.

Only Virtue is like the Phoenix: when it seems she is ending, she is reborn, turning opening applause into eternal veneration.

WHEN TO STRUT
YOUR STUFF

Envy sees better than 20/20, needs no reading glasses, and can penetrate into the distance, spotting a blemish invisible to Truth. She knows what regret is, and would be glad to see less than she does, for her vision gives her no rest. Peering through the eyes of all the birds, Envy alighted one day on that portent of beauty, that feathered sun, the Peacock, bird of Juno. The other birds gazed at him, and saw as many rays as the feathers in his showy fan.

From looking, one ascends to admiration, at least when there is no ill feeling. If there is, things spiral

---

* Gracián tells the story in *El Criticón*: Hercules helped Omphale knit a shirt, "a shroud for his reputation."

downward, and when it cannot turn into emulation, even a glance degenerates into the smallness of envy. The birds soon went blind from so much looking. The Jackdaw, vilest among them, having recently been stripped of his feathers, went croaking from one bird to the other: the Eagles on their cliffs, the Swans in their ponds, the Hawks on their perches, the Roosters on their dungheaps, and the Owls in their dark and gloomy attics.

He began with an artful bit of praise, and ended with scorn. "He's lovely, he's dazzling, this Peacock; who would deny it? A pity he's lost when he vaunts his beauty. For the finest qualities begin to seem trivial the moment one notices them in oneself. Self-praise is the surest form of censure. Those worth most have the least to say about themselves. If the Eagle were to fan his patriotic feathers, what do you think would happen? He'd steal the show with his majestic gravity. And don't we admire the Phoenix for fleeing from this sort of vulgar affectation, and keeping to her wise and legendary retirement?"

Those words planted envy in small hearts, which fill up easily with anything. For envy can stick to anything at all, even to what doesn't exist. Cruelest of emotions, which turns the good of others into sadness and venom. Unable to destroy the Peacock's beauty, the birds conspired to darken it. Adding subtlety to malice, they criticized not his loveliness but his vanity.

"If we can keep him from making such a show of his feathers," the Magpie said, "his beauty will go into a total eclipse."

What is not seen might not as well exist. Persius said it well: "Your knowledge is nothing if others do not know that you know." And all of the other gifts can take a hint, though he spoke only of their queen. Things are seldom taken for what they are, but for what they seem. There are more fools than intelligent people, and fools are content with appearances. Only the wise consider substance, and they are vastly outnumbered.

The Crow, the Jackdaw, the Magpie, and other ambassadors of the winged republic flew off to take the accusation to the Peacock. Others excused themselves: the Eagle because of his gravity, the Phoenix because no one could find her, the Dove because of her innocence, the Pheasant because he was too timid, and the Swan because he was lost in sweet, dreamy thought, preparing his final song.

In the luxurious palace of Wealth, they ran into the Parrot, who was on a balcony in a cage: the proper sphere of those who talk too much. The Parrot was glad to tell them as much as he knew, which was more than they wanted to hear. The Peacock was delighted to see them, for this was a new occasion to spread his feathers. He received them in a spacious courtyard, a stage for his showy splendor, where he could compete with the sun itself, day by day, ray for ray.

But this was the wrong moment for ostentation. It isn't always the right moment for excellence. Envy is a harpy, a basilisk: she claws at anything and kills with a glance. And though beauty can bewitch, today it merely turned applause into insult.

"You're getting what you deserve, you silly, pompous bird! We've brought an accusation from the entire winged senate. When you hear it, you're going to fold that fan of useless feathers and learn to be a little less conceited.

"Know that all birds are deeply offended by that presumptuous plumage. And they're right. Why do you alone, among all the birds, have to fan those silly feathers? No other bird even tries, though many could do it far better than you. Does the Crane show off its crest? Does the Ostrich let others see its plumage? Did you ever see the Phoenix show his sapphires and emeralds to the vulgar? You are hereby ordered, without possibility of appeal, to stop making yourself so singular. And believe me, it's for your own well-being. If your brain were a fraction as big as your fan, you would have noticed by now that the more you show off your feathers, the more you discover something very, very ugly!

"Ostentation is always vulgar, and always arises from vanity. It makes others hostile, and the wise give it no credit at all. Serious retirement, a prudent falling back, discretion, circumspection: all of these qualities are content to please only themselves. Reality is enough; it has no need for deceitful appearances and vain applause. And besides, you are the symbol of wealth. Is it smart, is it safe, to show your riches in public?"

Juno's lovely bird was amazed, and it took him a second to recover from confusion and emerge from his inner depths. "Why does praise always come from far away, and scorn come always from one's own? Can it really be that when I steal everyone's eyes, fastening them to my feathers, I am gossiped about by Magpies and Jackdaws? Which is it you are condemning, my beauty or my ostentation? Heaven told me both to *be* and *show*. What good would one be without the other? What use is reality without appearance? Our best politicians tell us that the best wisdom is to make things *seem*. To know, and to show you know, are double knowledge. What others say about luck is equally true of show: better an ounce of it than tons of riches without it. What good is being excellent if no one knows you are?

"What if the sun hid its brilliance, or the rose never left the prison of its bud, fanning itself into vivid color? What if the diamond, with the help of the jeweler, did not change its depths, and glimmerings and reflections? What would be the use of so much light, so much worth, so much beauty, without ostentation? I am a winged sun and a feathered rose and the jewel of nature, and when the heavens gave me perfection, they also expected me to show it off.

"The Maker of all creation thought of show before He thought of anything else. For He created light, and with it brilliance. And come to think of it, light was also the first thing He praised. Because light shows off everything else, He showed off light itself. So that from the very beginning, showing has been as important as being."

As he spoke, the Peacock put up his great shield of changing lights, as defensive about his beauty as he was offensive to Envy, who lost her head completely and led the birds' assault against him. The Raven went at his eyes, and all the rest at his feathers. The loveliest of all birds . . . cried out for help from heaven and earth . . . and other creatures came flying or running: the Lion, the Tiger, a Bear, two Monkeys . . .

The Lion asserted his authority, calmed them all down, and smiled when he heard what the rumpus was all about, telling one side to behave more modestly and the other to keep silent. After a few words he decided that Envy had no grounds for her complaints, but proposed that the case be remitted to the judgment of the Vixen, on account of her wisdom and her dispassionate nature. Both parties agreed to abide by her judgment.

The Vixen called on all her slyness in order to please everyone: to flatter the Lion without displeasing the Eagle; to do justice but not lose any friends.

"It is no easy thing to decide which matters more, reality or appearances. Some things are great in themselves but do not seem so, while others are little and seem much. Ostentation is as powerful as modesty. It can make up for what is missing, and if this is true of material things, for example in one's adornment and retinue, just think what it can do with the gifts of the spirit. When some fine quality is displayed just at the right moment, it's a triumph.

"There are people in whom what is little really shines, and what is much is enough to dazzle. When showiness combines with any sort of eminence, a prodigy is formed. We've all seen excellent people who lack that verve and style, and seem only half of themselves. Not many years ago, a great man terrified the world on the battlefield, but trembled and cringed in a staff meeting: he that could do much could say little. There are entire nations that are showy by nature, and here Spain is superior. In a word: ostentation is the very polish of heroical gifts. It gives them a second nature.

"But this is only true when it is backed up by reality. Where there is no merit, ostentation is vulgar deception, and all it does is to make defects more visible and laughable. Some people can't wait to show themselves on the universal stage, and once they get there, they show off only their ignorance, which had been hidden safely away.

"Nowhere do we have to be more careful of affectation than in displaying our gifts, for affectation borders on vanity, and vanity on scorn. Any show of talent must be moderate, and, as I was saying, it has to happen at just the right moment. Moderation in a matter like this is even more important than any sort of physical temperance . . .

"The wise sometimes display their gifts with a kind of dumb eloquence, as though by accident. And sometimes you can win applause by hiding your talents. The best display can be to hold things back, for privation stings the curiosity of others.

"It takes a certain grace to practice this art, and a certain slyness. It is a great stratagem not to reveal things all at once, and lay down your cards one by one, painting perfection with one stroke after another, suggesting it little by little, so that one gift seems to hint at another, greater one and heightens expectation. And the same is true of deeds, when you want to bait the admiration of others.

"And now, coming to the matter at hand, I say it would be violent to concede beauty to the Peacock and deny him permission to display it. Wise Nature would never agree to that, for she would be condemning her own providence. And no law should violate nature, except when reason overrules . . .

"Our remedy is both practical and efficient, and it is this. The Peacock is hereby commanded, each time he displays the variety and beauty of his plumage, to draw the eyes of others to his dreadfully ugly . . . well, feet. I can assure you that this alone will be enough to correct his vanity."

All applauded this sentence, the Peacock obeyed, and court was adjourned. They sent one of the birds to ask elegant, wise Aesop to add this modern incident to his ancient fables.

DON'T GIVE IN TO YOUR MOODS

Why is glorious Olympus the king of all mountains? Not because he towers over the very highest; for that is the duty of anything superior. Not because he allows himself to be seen from all sides; for greatness is always an object of imitation. Not because he is first to receive the rays of the sun; for majesty is naturally a center of brilliance. Not because he is crowned with stars; for primacy occupies, by definition, the summit of success. And not because his name is synonymous with heaven. But because he never submits to vulgar passing impressions, which is the greatest form of dominion over oneself. The winds kiss his feet, the clouds are his carpet, but they never rise any higher. And thus he never changes, and his eminence is alien to vulgar emotion.

A great talent never surrenders to changes in mood or allows its own peculiar temperament to run amok. It towers above such vulgar lack of composure. One of the great effects of wisdom is self-reflection, and if you can recognize your present disposition, you can master your own mind, conquer your moods, and not be dragged tyrannically from one sort of foolishness to another . . .

It shows great talent to foresee a mood and head it off, for this is an indisposition of the mind, and the wise behave toward this ailment as they do toward bodily ones. Sick people condemn nectar as bitter, but judgment corrects them, and thus should we correct our own vile moods and make allowance for our basic temperament, sometimes applying the opposite emotion, in order to balance the scales of prudence.

Some people are always limping on this or that side of their emotions: intolerable to those they deal with, odious stepfathers in any conversation, enemies of affability, spoiling every moment of good taste. Great gainsayers of themselves and others, attackers of all that is good, sponsors of anything foolish, questioners of whatever words anyone utters, sometimes only because someone else happened to cut the cards or deal the first hand. And if their interlocutor prudently yields, or takes their side so as to avoid something unseemly, they change to the opposite one, foiling even the discreet. There is less hope for them than for the truly mad; these, at least, can be humored; but with the stubborn no words suffice, no reasons can move those who do not reason at all . . .

When two of these stubborn, moody people bump into one another and go into battle, let the wise only watch, and not take part. I promise you much fun, if only you will retire behind the barriers and refrain from taking sides while they butt heads and lock horns.

It is no vulgarity to show your displeasure from time to time, when the occasion justifies it, and to feel a little out of tune. Never to be annoyed is to want always to be a beast. But chronic, incurable moodiness, before every sort of person, is unbearable and gross. The bitter pill slipped to you by, say, a servant need not affect your dealings with everyone else. But to check yourself, you have to know yourself.

In love with their own contradictions, the moody sniff out any excuse for a scrap, and come into conversation as though climbing into the ring. Insufferable harpies of good taste, who use both words and deeds as claws. And what if their vile mood strikes them with a half-understood book in their hands? How quickly they graduate from a B.A. in Arrogance to an M.A. in Malice! Sullen monsters of moodiness!

QUICKNESS OF WIT

Lightning was Jupiter's weapon of choice. He won his greatest victories with its sudden power. With bolts of lightning he cast down the rebel giants, for swiftness is the mother of success. They were transmitted by the eagle, for the gift of quickness is always delivered on the wings of a soaring mind.

Some people excel at quick thinking, others at quick doing. The former please, the latter astonish.

"Soon enough if well enough," said the Sage. We never examine the quickness or slowness of a work, only its perfection. This alone governs our esteem, for speed is a mere circumstance, either ignored or forgotten, and success alone endures. To the contrary: what was done quickly will as soon be undone; finished as fast as it was finished. What must last an eternity takes an eternity to make.

But if all successes deserve admiration, quick ones deserve applause: they double eminence. Some people think much and later err in everything; others think nothing and hit the mark immediately. A lively wit can substitute for depth of judgment, and prevent others from taking counsel. For these people there is no "perhaps." Their unfailing wit is a stand-in for providence.

Offhand remarks can beguile taste, charm admiration, and capture applause. A spontaneous trifle is often better than excellence foreseen. Charles V spoke wisely, without saying very much: "Time and I are a match for any two." More to the point was another maxim: "He has no time, but mine is any!"* Whoever says time says everything: counsel, foresight, occasion, maturity, delay, assure success. But spontaneous deeds and thoughts are insured only by quickness and good luck.

Even when providence foresees and prudence arranges and occasion assists, execution often aborts. In order to give birth to success, quickness needs less assistance. She has only luck and courage, and she seems especially excellent in the light of mistaken counsel.

Some attribute these quick successes to luck alone. But they also require an astonishing clear-sightedness. This gift of heroes owes nothing to art and everything to nature. There can be no artifice where attentiveness scarcely has time to help and where

---

* The meaning appears to be: He can never find the right occasion ("time"), but for me any occasion is the right one.

inspiration leaves no room for thought. What quickness makes use of is presence of mind and self-control, and the grace and composure that rise above confusion. Reigning over difficulty and over herself, quickness does not come and see and conquer; she conquers and sees and comes.

She tests her liveliness in the very tightest situations, and her intelligence thrives on opposition. Danger often makes people braver; difficulty sharpens their sight and their wits. There are those who reason best when they have the least time. The greater the risk, the more impressive their escape, for there is often a certain something,* in those situations, that makes intelligence more intense, wit more subtle, and prudence more substantial.

There are monstrous heads who get everything right spontaneously and everything wrong when they think. Some think of everything at once, and nothing thereafter: no use advising counsel or appealing to "later." Not that it harms them: wise Nature gave them quickness instead of thought, and trusting in her, they fear no circumstance.

Quick-witted sayings, quick-footed deeds. One alone was enough to make Solomon the greatest of

---

* Gracián calls it, pedantically, "antiparastasis": the rhetorical figure with which the accused holds that what he is accused of is praiseworthy. Modernity would call it "adrenaline."

the wise, and was more formidable than all his success and power. Another two made Alexander and Caesar the firstborns of fame. One cut the Gordian knot, and the other rose by falling.* Quickness gave them each a part of the world and tested their ability to govern.

Spontaneity in speech is commendable, but quickness in acts deserves applause. A quick, happy effect suggests an energetic cause, subtlety in thought, shrewdness in getting things right. And quickness grows even more estimable as it graduates from cleverness to prudence, from wit to good judgment.

A gift like this accredits heroes and suggests great depth and great heights of talent. How often we admired it in that great hero, our protector, the most excellent Duke of Nocera, Francesco Maria Carafa, with his prodigious contexture of talents and deeds. Luck was able to cut its threads, but not stain it with the envy of the times he lived in. He showed the greatest possible leadership in the most desperate causes, perfect tranquility in reasoning, clarity in execution, a stylish ease in all he did, and quickness in his successes. Where others shrugged their shoulders, he thrust out his hands. Nothing was too sud-

---

* Caesar stumbled and fell when he touched African soil, but saved face, exclaiming, "I hereby take possession of you!"

den for his attention, too dark for his sharp sight. His wittiness rivaled his prudence, and although luck deserted him in the end, fame never did.*

In generals and athletes, this is the best of all advantages, for almost all their actions are unforeseen, and their execution immediate. They have no time to study the occasion or defend themselves from chance. They seize opportunity, triumph with alacrity, fly toward victory.

Among rulers, meditation brings more credit, for all their acts are eternal. They think for many, helping themselves with auxiliary wits, and many things must come together for universal success. They have time, and a bed where they ripen their decisions; a day of success takes nights of thought, and they exercise their heads more than their hands.

---

* Francesco Maria Carafa, Duke of Nocera (1579–1642), whom Gracián had served as confessor, died in prison after being charged with collaborating with the French.

BE FULLY A PERSON

*A Dialogue Between the Author
and Dr. Manuel Salinas y Linaza,
Canon of the
Holy Church at Huesca*

AUTHOR: It was a striking peculiarity of the Persians not to want to see their children until they were seven years old. Even paternal love, the greatest of all, did not blind them to the imperfections of childhood. They did not count them as their children until they were able to reason.

SALINAS: If a parent cannot suffer his own ignorant little child, and if reason waits seven years to admit him to her communication, why should it surprise us that an intelligent person cannot tolerate a fool and banishes him from his learned familiarity?

AUTHOR: Nature, wisely provident, does not allow things to reach perfection in a single day, and neither does the diligence of art. They advance one day at a time until they reach fullness.

SALINAS: All beginnings are small, even those of

very large things. Only gradually do they reach the muchness of perfection. Things perfected in a moment are worth little and last less. A flower is as soon made as unmade. But diamonds are forever because they took that long to be formed.

AUTHOR: And the same is true of people. Each day they perfect themselves, both in character and in morals, until they reach fullness of good judgment, ripeness of taste, the perfection of a consummate personality.

SALINAS: You're right, for each day we meet people who reason and know but are not fully made. They lack a certain something, sometimes what is best. Intensity advances by degrees. Some are at the very beginnings of intelligence, but they will learn. Others are ahead in everything; and still others have reached the consummation of their gifts . . . Like wine coming slowly to maturity, the mind grows more perfect each day in the fragile vessel of the body. All people have, in their beginnings, the annoying sweetness of childhood, the tartness and rawness of youth; an excessive fondness for pleasure; an inclination toward playful, frivolous occupations. And though we get a hint of maturity in the rare few, it is far from the full savor of time. A certain seriousness, natural or affected, tries to conceal the imperfections of youth. But soon, in a playful slip, it confirms that it has not yet reached the point of perfection.

AUTHOR: Time is a great healer because of its age and experience.

SALINAS: It alone can heal one of youth, which is truly an ailment. With age, thoughts grow greater and more elevated, taste more distinguished; the wit is purified; judgment and will come to ripeness; and at last the entire person, in all his fullness, is pleasant enough to join the company of the learned. He comforts with his advice, warms with his efficiency, delights with his reasoning, and is fragrant with noble generosity.

AUTHOR: But before they come into season, what harshness people bring to things! How grating they are on the understanding, how harsh in dealing with others, how ungainly in their movements!

SALINAS: And what a torment it is for maturity and wisdom to have to adjust to someone unseasoned and unmade! A torment worse than the one dreamed up by Phalaris,* who tied a living man to a dead one, hand to hand and cheek to jowl.

AUTHOR: Once someone has reached a certain wisdom, he goes back over his imperfections, recognizes the stains left by ignorance or rashness,

---

* Sicilian tyrant (sixth century B.C.), whose cruelty was legendary.

takes his bad taste to trial, and laughs at himself judiciously and self-reflectively, condemning the faults that his emotions led him into.

SALINAS: Sadly, some are never fully made.

AUTHOR: Some piece is always missing, some part of taste (which is bad) or judgment (which is worse).

SALINAS: But more often, that missing piece is impossible to define.

AUTHOR: I have noticed, also, that Time brings everyone to maturity at a different pace.

SALINAS: Sometimes he flies, and at others he is lame. Sometimes uses his wings and sometimes his crutches. There are some who come quickly to perfection in any matter, and others who take time to do so, doing universal harm, as when responsibility is involved. And people grow not only in the pursuit of prudence but also in each job, each state, each occupation.

AUTHOR: And what about kings?

SALINAS: Even kings are born unmade. Great matter for prudence and experience! A thousand perfections go into the fullness of majesty. A general is made not only from his own blood but also from that of others; an orator, after much study and learning; even a doctor sends a hundred people to the grave before he allows one to rise from his bed. All make themselves gradually till they reach their point of perfection.

AUTHOR: And is that point a fixed one?

SALINAS: That is the price we pay for inconstancy. There is no happiness, because on earth there is no fixed star, no state of rest, only continuous change. All waxes and wanes, crazy and inconstant.

AUTHOR: The moral world follows the natural one, and with age the memory and understanding begin to decay.

SALINAS: And that makes it all the more important to take advantage of their best moments, and to know how to enjoy things at their fullest.

AUTHOR: Much is required to climb to the summit of perfection.

SALINAS: Vulcan hammers away before the gods deign to inhabit a statue, and the favors of nature require cultivation, effort, and continual contact with the wise, both the living and the dead, through books and conversation. Faithful experience, judicious observation, the continual going over of matters that are sublime, a variety of occupations and pursuits: all these things help produce the consummate person, ripe and perfect, accurate in judgment, mature in taste, attentive in speech, wise in sayings, shrewd in deeds, the center of all perfection.

AUTHOR: There is nothing more precious than a person in his season.

SALINAS: We should seek him as a friend, use him as an advisor, oblige him as a protector, and beseech him to be our teacher.

THE GENEALOGY OF REFINEMENT

Your father was Artifice, the teacher of Nature. You were born under his tutelage so that you could bring everything to perfection. Without you the greatest deeds come to nothing, and the best works lose their luster. We have seen people who were prodigiously intelligent and inventive, but so inelegant that they reaped more scorn than applause.

The most learned and gravest sermon is insipid without your grace; the weightiest argument, useless without your economy; the most erudite book, shunned without your polish; and, in a word, the rarest invention, best choice, deepest learning, and sweetest eloquence are condemned, without you, as common, shallow, barbarous, and unmemorable.

There are many who, when we examine them

carefully, have no great wit or depth or any other fine quality and yet are praised merely for their finesse and their sense of order. Your perfection is transcendental: it affects all of the other gifts. With your help, ugliness has often conquered beauty. For perfection sometimes grows overconfident, and self-confidence often leads to defeat. The showier the talent, the more one notices disorder and neglect: talent itself calls attention to inelegance. In a word: with you, what is little seems much; and without you, much seems nothing at all.

Your mother was wise Arrangement, who assigns each thing to its proper place and composes a harmonious whole. Everything in nature suffers violence when removed from its proper resting place, and everything artificial is thrown into confusion. A star shines more brightly in one house than in another . . . Where there is sloppiness and disorder, sublime invention labors in vain, and so do subtle reasoning, studiousness, selection, and wide learning.

Even saintliness should be comely and neat and well ordered, and builds twice as much with the help of religious urbanity. Holiness is no less holy for being neat, no less wise . . .

Not only the understanding but the will, too, should be well ordered. Let these two superior powers be refined; and if knowledge ought to show neat-ness and polish, why should desire be barbarous and gross?

Your sisters were Good Taste, Decorum, and Grace, which beautify everything, bringing it to maturity . . .

How gross and disorderly and uncouth the world was before learned Greece introduced refinement, spreading her finesse with her empire. The Greeks brought refinement to their cities, and not only to buildings but also to citizens. They believed other nations barbarous, and they were right. They invented the three orders of architecture for the adornment of their temples and palaces, and cultivated the sciences in their schools. Refinement made them fully people.

The Romans, through the greatness of their spirit and power, extended their refinement along with their sovereignty. They emulated and surpassed the Greeks, nearly expelling barbarity from the world, making it more refined and cleaner in every possible way. There are still traces of that greatness and refinement in some buildings, and when common people ponder the excellence of something, they call it an *obra de romanos*, "a work of Romans." The same skill and artifice are found in some statues, where the rare skill of the sculptor eternalizes the fame of the heroes portrayed. Even in their coins and seals one can admire that meticulousness, for they expected all objects to be beautiful and showed total intolerance for barbarism . . .

Where Roman culture and decorum reach their extremes is in the immortal works of her prodigious writers. The ingeniousness of her writers competes with the courage of her doers. Valiant hearts, valiant minds!

Some provinces still bear traces of this hereditary order and refinement, especially learned Italy, the center of that empire. All of her cities are neat and well ordered, both in their government and in their economies. In Spain, refinement is found more in individuals than in public buildings. Not that this is praise, for wherever it is found, barbarity is barbarity, and it detracts from one's reputation. In France, refinement flourishes, reaching extremes of gallantry, at least among nobles. The arts are esteemed, letters are venerated, and gallantry, courtesy, and discretion have reached perfection. The noblest citizens count themselves the best read and best informed, for nothing brings refinement like knowledge . . .

Your children are Advancement and Pleasure. In a garden what most beguiles us, besides the way in which the plants and flowers were selected, is the way they are arranged, and the same is true, to an even greater extent, in the garden of the spirit, where we admire the fragrance of wise sayings, the gallantry of deeds, both made more striking by refinement.

Some people are naturally neat and elegant: order and cleanliness seem to emanate from them by some secret force, and their hearts are impatient with any sort of disorder. Even when dealing with soldiers, Alexander sought refinement. Quintus Curtius* tells us that his troops seemed more like orders of neat senators than lines of unruly men. But there are others with hearts in disarray where there is no room for either care or artifice. All that they do carries the stigma of sloppiness and the unmistakable signs of barbarism.

Refinement is an accident that suggests substance, is born from talent, and shows up in even the commonest things. A Japanese† once built a fire so neatly that he rose from servant to emperor. Fortune worked a miracle, turning kindling into a scepter . . .

---

* The author of a history of Alexander the Great (ca. A.D. 42).

† Gracián identifies him as "Taikosama." Romera-Navarro believes he is referring to Toyotomi Hideyoshi (1537–1598).

JUDICIOUS AND
OBSERVANT

Momus, god of censure and scorn, was very vulgar indeed the day he called for a little opening in the human breast, the better to observe the feelings of others. He should have known that the readers of the human heart need no crack to get into even the most reserved of people. Those who can use a telescope have no use for such a window. People who know their own minds have a key that can unlock any heart.

The person who is judicious and observant can master any subject and any object. An Argos of attention, a lynx who can penetrate the darkest intentions, he searches bosoms for dissimulation, and expertly measures the volume of any talent. He flushes the ignoramus from his protective silence, and discerns a hypocrite against the whiteness of someone's sepulchre. He discovers, takes critical note, understands, and comprehends, defining each thing according to its essence.

Every great person is judicious, and every judicious person great, for this is a dimension of intelligence that is itself the highest of gifts. It is good to be knowledgeable, but not enough. You must also be judicious. A critic must be excellent himself to give value to the things he appraises. He examines objects and graduates subjects, neither admiring nor despising everything, but meting out his esteem to each.

He distinguishes immediately between reality and appearances, for a real talent takes command of objects before they take hold of his intelligence or his desire. There are diviners of the understanding who know how to peer inside things and not stop on the surface, where, sometimes, all that glitters is vulgar gold.

Their intelligence throws critical light on objects, discerning the true from the false. They are great decipherers of intentions and purposes, and they can crack any code of dissimulation. Deceit can boast few victories over them; ignorance, even fewer.

Tacitus mastered this skill with respect to individuals; Seneca, with respect to all mankind.

No gift could be further from vulgarity, and this one alone can certify someone as wise; for the crowd has always been malicious but not judicious, and though it says everything, the reach of its understanding is short. Only rarely, in its ignorance and error, does it discern between what is apparent and what is real. Most people bite only at the bark, and feel no nausea when they swallow deceit.

How wonderful it is to see one of these appraisers of talent, these uncoverers of depths, as he gains ground on someone else. When two judicious people, equally armed with attentiveness and caution, attack one another, each tries to measure the other's talent. How skillfully they attack, how adroitly they feint! How attentive they are to words and motives! They turn over their cards one by one, gauging the emotions, assaying prudence. They are taken in neither by two successes, for this could have been luck, nor by two witty remarks, for they might have been memorized.

They chart one another's minds, and test one another's talents. There is no hawk who feints like this before his prey. No Argos can multiply into as many eyes. They take the entire anatomy of their opponent, from head to heart, and can define him in a second, according to his properties and his essence.

It is a great pleasure to meet, and to defeat, one of these masters, who open up only in the confidence of friendship. They are quick to censure others but slow to criticize them publicly, and they use another great stratagem: feel with the few and speak with the many. But when, assured of the friendship of their listener, they turn their backs to the fray and share their observations, what things can be learned from them! They place each person in the right category, find the breaking point for each action, praise each maxim, weigh each fact, discover the truth in anything. One hardly knows what to admire more in them: their singular caution, the subtlety and depth of their observation, the accuracy of their judgments, the boldness of their conceptions, the prudence of their reasoning, the much that occurs to them, or the little that escapes their notice.

The surest eminences tremble before them, and lay their own satisfaction aside, for their judgment is an infallible touchstone of refinement. The gift that earns their approval can show itself anywhere it wants, for it has been rightly judged, and not by the fickleness of the crowd, whose applause is more noise than discernment. The idols of common people are often unable to survive the first rush of reputation, and are quickly cast down. A quiet "yes" from one of these brave judges is worth more than any sort of public acclamation. It was not for nothing that Plato called Aristotle his entire school, and Antigone spoke of Zeno as the entire "portrait" of his fame.

This most valiant of gifts pulls others into its sphere: understanding, knowledge, sharpness, depth.

And it repels others: credulity, strange notions, whimsical reasoning. For it is made of strength and constancy and deliberation.

But notice how different it is to censure and to gossip; for judgment implies indifference, and gossip a predisposition toward malice. The staunchest of censors celebrates the good as easily as he condemns the bad, drawing upon funds of equity and dispassion. This aphorism does not bid the prudent to be cynical, but to be intelligent and observant. It advises them neither to censure everything—for this would be an abominable and moody lack of moderation—nor to applaud everything, which is pedantry. There are some who find only the bad in things, sniffing it out amid much that is good. They conceive like vipers, through the mouth, and burst when they give birth: just punishment for the meanness of their spirits. It is one thing to be a Momus of bad taste, battening oneself on what is rotten; quite another to be an upright Cato, a lover of fairness, a model of integrity.

These judicious, observant people are oracles of truth, dispassionate judges of merit, but they keep to themselves, and rub shoulders only with other prudent people, for truth cannot be trusted to malice or to ignorance. But whenever—what bliss!—two of them communicate their feelings, judgments, reasoning, and information, it is a moment worthy to be dedicated to the Muses, the Graces, and Minerva.

This kind of prudence finds it as easy to do as to speculate, above all in those who have positions of authority. They use its light to discover the right talent for each position, weigh people's merits for rewards, and take the pulse of their character and intelligence. They can arrange any matter because they comprehend everything. They select with art, not by luck. It takes them only a second to discover someone's strengths and weaknesses, eminence or mediocrity, what might be improved, and what should be toned down. Personal affection has no room here, and neither do emotion and deceit, the Scylla and Charybdis of success. For the one leads to self-deception, and the other is a wish to be deceived by others. These people are also the staunchest judges of reason. Like Justice herself, they see without eyes and feel without hands.

How precious is freedom of judgment, ruled neither by common ignorance nor by any sort of favoritism. All belongs to truth, though sometimes for safety and sometimes out of affection, the wise want to take truth into their own bosoms, keeping her all to themselves.

Besides being a delight, this great gift—judiciousness—does something of incalculable importance: it helps select intimate friends, discerning between the prudent and the foolish, the unique and the vulgar. Just as the greatest strategy in cards is to know which ones to lay down, the greatest rule for living is to know which people make a winning hand.

The author heard these words from an oracle: from the deepest and greatest understanding of them all, the Duke of Híjar. These teachings are but an echo of his instruction.

A PLEASANT MANNER

For this great precept Cleobulus was ranked first among the Seven Sages. And therefore, it is the first of precepts. If merely teaching it made him renowned for his wisdom, what is left for those who practice it? To know things but not practice them is to be not a philosopher but a grammarian.

Things have no less need of circumstance than of substance. In fact, what we run into first aren't essences but appearances. We begin knowing from the outside in. From the rind of behavior we judge the fruits of talent. We judge even the person we do not know by his bearing.

A good manner is one of the subtle gifts of merit. Because it can be acquired, it is inexcusable to lack it. In some it is a natural gift, helped along by artifice; and in others it is entirely a creation of art; for art can remedy nature's acts of forgetfulness, and more than make up for her lapses. And when both art and nature combine, they produce an agreeable, successful person.

It is also one of the transcendental beauties that affect all actions and employments. Truth is strong, reason brave, justice powerful, but it takes a fine manner to make them shine. It compensates for any fault, even those of reason, gilding the iron of error, applying makeup to the face of ugliness, correcting awkwardness, and dissimulating all other defects.

How many serious, important things have fallen victim to bad manners, and how many desperate things have been rescued by good ones!

A minister's zeal, a leader's courage, a scholar's knowledge, a prince's power, are never enough unless accompanied by this most important of formal qualities. It is the political adornment of scepters, the jewel in any crown, and in fact it plays its most important role in leadership. It makes others feel obliged, for superiors achieve more through their humanity than through despotism. To see a prince lay aside his superiority and behave with humaneness and courtesy makes others feel doubly indebted to him. One must reign in people's hearts to govern their wills. It doesn't matter whether this courtesy is natural or artificial: either way, people applaud it and enjoy it.

There are things more esteemed for their manner than for their being. A good manner can give novelty to the past, bring it back, and give it another turn. When circumstances are right, they refute the weariness of old age. Taste is always moving forward, never turns round, never bites at what has passed, but always nibbles on novelty. It can be taken in by style and charm. Things are freshened up by circumstance, and there are ways to disguise the staleness and ennui of things often repeated. This is especially true of all sorts of imitation, which never attains the striking sublimity of what comes first.

It is true, also, in matters of wit. For even when things are well known, the speaker can present them, the historian write them, in a new, more appetizing way.

When things are exquisite, it tires no one to hear them repeated six or seven times. But though they do not annoy, they awaken no admiration unless they're presented in a new way, and hit us with a new aroma. Novelty is always welcome. It tickles the taste.

Change the seasoning and you will renew things: a great secret for giving pleasure.

How many vulgar, ordinary things have been turned into something new and excellent, and bartered for taste and admiration. And, to the contrary, how many choice things, without this spice, have fallen by the wayside of pleasure!

A pleasant manner takes pride in its discretion. With the very same things one man will flatter, another will batter our ears. The "how" is everything: the right word or deed, in just the right way. And if a lack of grace is condemnable, what of the deliberately unpleasant manner that is sometimes affected by people who deal with many others? Affectation, arrogance, rudeness, impatience, and other parallel monsters make many people all but unapproachable. A wise man once remarked that to go around scowling is to ruin a whole life with a tiny gesture. Whereas an agreeable expression promises an agreeable character; and a lovely one, gentleness within.

Above all, take pains to gild your "no," so that it will be even more valued than a bitter "yes." Good manners sweeten truth so skillfully that they pass it off as flattery. Sometimes you can turn an unpleasant truth into a compliment. You tell people not what they are but what they ought to be.

This is the one sure refuge for people who lack talent. They can accomplish more with their pleasant manner than others with all their natural perfection. It makes up for one's defects in any occupation, high or low, and will never be defined or pinned down, for no one knows what it consists of; or perhaps we should say that it is the Three Graces together, in a composite of all perfection . . .

AN ART FOR BEING FORTUNATE

Fortune, who is always in disguise, has many who complain about her, and few who feel gratitude. This general discontent reaches even the beasts (and who better?). The one complaining loudest was the simplest of them all. He was moving from one gossipy group to another, awakening not only compassion but applause, especially from the vulgar.

Advised by many, accompanied by none, he presented himself one day in the general audience of the sovereign Jupiter. With profound humility (how welcome in any fool!), he asked permission to be heard, and delivered this badly arranged little speech:

"Oh candid Jupiter (and please be just, and not vengeful): before you, in your majestic presence, lies the most unhappy, most ignorant of brutes, asking not redress for the wrongs done to me but remedy for my misfortune. How is it, O eternal god, that you allow your strength to be administered by impious Fortune, who is blind only to me, and who behaves like a tyrant or a stepmother. Why does she torment *me*, the simplest of animals? I can endure the charge of stupidity, but why should cruel Fortune add the surcharge of misfortune? Trampling on common custom, she both makes me a fool and makes me unhappy, persecuting innocence and favoring malice. The proud lion triumphs, and so do the cruel tiger, the sly vixen, and the ravenous wolf. I alone, who do no harm to anyone, am harmed by all. I eat little and work a great deal: a short carrot and a very long stick. I look unkempt and ugly, even to myself, and can't go out among people, and the worst indignity of all is having to pull the carts of peasants from one place to another."

All present were deeply moved by this sorry proclamation. All except grave Jupiter, who is not so vulgarly persuaded. He was lying on his side, resting his head on his arm: not so much out of weariness as to cover one ear, reserving it for the other side of the story. "Call Fortune," he said.

Soldiers and students and pretenders went scurrying off to look for her, covered much ground, and found her nowhere. They entered the house of powerful Command, but people were moving so confusedly, with such haste and so little reason, that they found no one to answer them, or even listen. They reflected that Fortune probably had little to do with such confusion, and they were right. They knocked at the door of Wealth, and Worry told them that Fortune had been there, but had stayed only long enough to order some bundles of thorns and sacks of needles. They ran into a fool, asked no questions, and went on to the house of Wisdom. Poverty came to the door and said that she wasn't there either, but was expected any day.

Only one house was left, and it stood alone, at the end of a narrow path. The door was closed, but they knocked, and were received by a maiden so lovely they believed her to be one of the Graces. She told them, very pleasantly, that she was Virtue. As they spoke, Fortune emerged from deep in the house, smiling. They served her Jupiter's subpoena, and she obeyed, as she usually does, flying off blindly to look for him.

Reverently she approached the sacred throne, and everyone bowed and curtsied. "What's going on, Fortune?" asked Jupiter. "I have people complaining every day about your behavior. I know how hard it is to please most people, how impossible to please all. I'm also aware that most do badly because they do well, and instead of being grateful for the much that they have, they complain about the little that they lack. When they look at someone else, they see only his sack of good luck, and when they look at themselves, only their sack of misfortunes. They see the luster of a crown, but not its weight or its worries. And therefore I pay no attention to their whining, or haven't until now; but the complaints of this poor wretch have some semblance of truth."

Fortune stole a glance at him and began to smile, but, remembering where she was, checked herself and said with composure, "Supreme Jupiter, a single word will be my excuse, and it is this: if he is an *ass*, who is he complaining about?" All laughed, and Jove himself applauded and instructed the asinine accuser:

"Miserable brute, you wouldn't be so unfortunate if you were just a little sharper. Go forth and try, from today on, to be as alert as the lion, as prudent as the elephant, as clever as the fox, as crafty as the wolf. Take thought for how you get there and you'll get what you want. And let all mortals take a lesson: the only luck, the only misfortune, are wisdom and folly."

WISE DISTRIBUTION
OF THE LIFE OF
THE DISCREET

The wise measure out their lives as though they had both a short and a long time to live. Life without a rest is like a long day's journey without an inn . . . Nature herself attentively proportioned the life of man to the path of the sun, and the four ages to the four seasons of the year.

Spring begins in childhood, all tender flowers and fragile hopes.

Then comes the feverish Summer of youth, dangerous in every way, with its burning blood and storms of emotion.

Next comes the yearned-for Autumn of maturity, crowned with the ripe fruits of judgment, maxims, and success.

All comes to an end in the frozen Winter of old age. The leaves of valor fall to the ground, white hair appears like snow, the streams of the veins are frozen, teeth and hair disappear, and life shivers and trembles in the presence of death. This was the way that Nature combined seasons and ages.

And Nature's rival, Art, tries to distribute moral life in a somewhat similar manner, giving it an ingenious variety. Pythagoras said it in a word, or rather in a single letter, Y, whose two branches symbolize the paths of good and evil. They say that Hercules came at dawn to this parting of the ways, for reason is an aurora and here he felt confusion. He looked at the path on the right with fear, and the one on the left with affection. The first was narrow and difficult, all uphill, and little traveled. The other was spacious and easy, gently sloping, and often used. He stopped here and studied until a hand from above guided him impulsively down the path of virtue to the resting place of heroism.

Some have written—among them the great Falcó,* whose singing made him a swan—that man was given thirty years of his own, in which to enjoy himself; twenty, lent from the Mule, in which to work; another twenty from the Dog, in which to bark; and twenty years from the Monkey, in which to grow old and die: an excellent fable, full of truth.

Another elegantly divided the comedy into three acts, and the voyage of life into three seasons. The

---

* The Valencian poet and mathematician Jaume Joan Falcó (1522–1594).

first he used to speak with the dead; the second, with the living; the third, with himself.

Let us decipher the enigma.

He destined the first third of his life to books and reading, which were more enjoyment than toil. For if a person is more of one the more he knows, the noblest of all occupations will be learning. He devoured books, nourishment for the soul and a delight to the spirit. What great happiness it was to meet the select few in each subject! He learned all of the arts worthy of a noble mind, as opposed to the ones written for those enslaved to work.

He prepared himself, at great pains, with a precise knowledge of languages: the two universal ones, Latin and Spanish, which, today, are the keys of the world; as well as Greek, Italian, French, English, and German, in order to enjoy the much good that has become eternal in them.

He gave himself next to the great mother of life, spouse of the understanding, and daughter of experience, laudable History, the art that most delights and most teaches. He began with the ancients and ended with the moderns, though others do the opposite. He spared neither histories of his own nation nor those of foreign ones, both sacred and profane, and he selected carefully, appraising each author and distinguishing between times, periods, centuries, and eras, with a broad understanding of monarchies, republics, and empires, with their increases, declines, and changes; the number, order, and quality of their princes; their deeds in war and in peace—and all this with so fine a memory that he seemed a spacious stage for ever-present antiquity.

He strolled through the delightful gardens of Poetry, not so much to use it as to study it, which is beneficial and becoming. He was neither so ignorant that he was unable to write a poem, nor so rash as to write two. He read all of the true poets, sharpening his wits with their maxims and ripening his judgment with their wisdom, and, among all of them, he devoted his bosom to profound Horace and gave a hand—his own—to Martial, delivering both of them by heart to the understanding. To poetry he joined the other Humanities and letters, storing up a treasure of erudition.

He went on to Philosophy, and beginning with Natural, came to the causes of things, the composition of the universe, the elegance and intricacy of the human body, the properties of animals, the virtues of herbs, and the qualities of precious stones. He found more enjoyment in Moral Philosophy, nourishment of those who are truly people, in order to give life to wisdom, and he pursued that wisdom in the sages and philosophers who bequeathed it to us in adages, aphorisms, emblems, and fables. He was a great disciple and ideal reader of Seneca, and an impassioned one of the divine Plato; a student of the Seven Sages, of Epictetus, and of Plutarch; and he did not disdain the useful and lovely Aesop.

He studied Cosmography, both physical and mathematical, measuring the lands and seas, distinguishing places and climates; the four parts of the universe; and in them the provinces and nations, kingdoms and republics, at times only to know and at times to speak about them, so as not to be numbered among the vulgar, whose ignorance or laziness keeps them from ever knowing where their feet are resting.

He learned as much of Astrology as wisdom permits. He recognized the celestial bodies, noted their various movements, numbered the stars and planets, and observed their influences and effects.

He crowned this practical studiousness with a continual, serious reading of Holy Scripture, the most beneficial and various of reading, and most agreeable to the taste of that great Phoenix among kings, Alfonso the Magnanimous, who read the entire Bible fourteen times, in the midst of so many, and such heroic, occupations.

With all this he achieved a knowledgeable universality, so that Moral Philosophy made him prudent;

Natural, wise; History, cautious; Poetry, ingenious; Rhetoric, eloquent; the Humanities, discreet; Cosmography, well informed; Holy Scripture, reverent; and all of them together, consummate. This was the great first act of his life.

He spent the second in pleasant travels. Here, too, is happiness for a person who is curious and observant. He searched out and enjoyed all that is good and better in the world, for to enjoy things fully one must see and not merely imagine them, and those who see things only once take more delight in them than those who see them often. For enjoyment is often threatened by continuity: the first day, an object delights its owner, and after that, only others can be surprised.

He turned over the entire universe, and promenaded through all of its political provinces: wealthy Spain, populous France, lovely England, crafty Germany, brave Poland, pleasant Moscow, and all of this together in Italy. He admired their most famous gathering places, seeking in each city whatever was notable, both old and modern: magnificent temples, sumptuous buildings; efficient governments; wise inhabitants, lustrous nobles, learned scholars; refined behavior.

He frequented the courts of the greatest princes,

enjoying all manner of prodigies natural and artistic, in paintings, statues, tapestries, libraries, jewels, arms, gardens, and museums.

He communicated with the first and best people in the world, those eminent in arms or letters or the arts, esteeming any sign of excellence. And all this with judicious comprehension, noting, censuring, comparing, and assigning to each thing its proper worth.

The third act of such a lovely life, the best and greatest, he spent in meditating upon all that he had read and, even more, upon all that he had seen. Everything that comes through the doors of the senses must pass through the custom house of understanding. There all is searched through and examined. Now he ponders, judges, reasons, infers, and tries to extract the essences of things. He has swallowed all he has read, devoured all he has seen, and now he ruminates, breaking down his nourishment and inquiring into truth, so that his spirit can better nourish itself on genuine wisdom.

The age of maturity is destined to contemplation, for the soul acquires strength as the body loses it, and the superior part of us grows stronger as the inferior decays. In maturity, one forms a very different concept of things, for both reason and the emotions come into season. Often we can look back prudently and see fully what we merely glimpsed during our youth.

Seeing makes us knowledgeable, but contemplation makes us wise. All of the old philosophers traveled, exploring first with their eyes and feet, but later with their intelligence, and this is what made them so rare. The crown of discretion is to know how to philosophize, drawing from everything, like the solicitous bee, either the honey of usefulness and fine taste, or wax for the candles of disillusionment. Philosophy itself is nothing but a meditation upon death: we must think about it often to do it well but once.